Helen Philipps'
CROSS STITCH
Garden Notebook

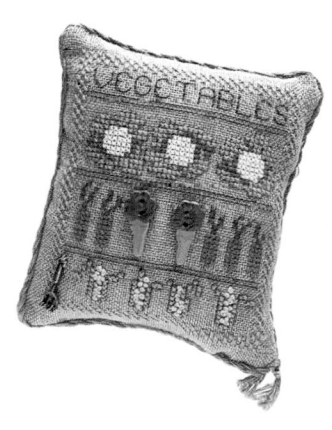

HELEN PHILIPPS'
CROSS STITCH
Garden Notebook

David & Charles

For my parents, who taught me the joys of gardening

(Picture on page 2)
A selection of attractive garden signs, quick to stitch and easy to work
on stitching paper — see pages 26 and 27

A DAVID & CHARLES BOOK

First published in the UK in 2001

A catalogue record for this book is available from the British Library.

ISBN 0 7153 1013 5

Project editing and charts by Linda Clements
Book design by Diana Knapp and Margaret Foster
Printed in Italy by LEGO SpA
for David & Charles
Brunel House   Newton Abbot   Devon

CONTENTS

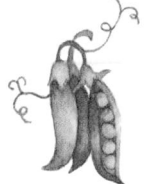

INTRODUCTION

The idea for a cross stitch garden notebook came to me when I was looking through one of my design ideas books. I have long kept notebooks and scrapbooks full of snippets, quotations, ideas, drawings and cuttings. I even include things like pressed flowers, small shells, coloured paper, fabric and threads. I thought that a garden notebook in cross stitch would be an interesting idea and imagined it with decorative pages filled with garden lore, cross stitch pictures and watercolour images.

There were many garden elements that I could cover as the subject is such a rich mixture. I wanted to give a flavour of some of the different kinds of gardens, especially my own favourites, so I included chapters on cottage gardens, kitchen gardens, formal gardens and herb gardens. I also wanted to illustrate some of my favourite decorative vegetables, flowers and fruits, so in went peas, pansies, lavender, strawberries – and many more. Bees and beehives have their own sampler, while other garden visitors are remembered with projects featuring birds, butterflies and insects. My love of topiary trees is also reflected in the book, the solid form of topiary lending itself beautifully to cross stitch designing.

In creating the book I also drew on the fact that gardeners have a great store of folklore and advice, passed on from one generation to the next and these were drawn on to add interesting snippets to the pages. You could feature some of them in your work as I have done, designing projects which include folklore, poetry and plant recipes in their designs. There are so many intriguing garden proverbs that it was difficult to choose a limited number. I have certainly learnt all kinds of interesting gardening advice, some of which make perfect sense – some a little less so!

One of the other features of this book is my use of embellishments in the form of buttons, charms and beads. They are sometimes the inspiration for a design and work particularly well for a garden theme. There is a section devoted to their use on the following pages.

The main point of this book is to have fun stitching little projects and larger samplers with a garden theme, to enjoy making them to keep or to give as treasured gifts. I think I have managed to include a little of everything and have learnt much more about gardening in the process. It has been a delightful book to work on and I hope it will give people who love stitching and gardening as much pleasure as it has given me.

The fresh, bright colours of the Apple Tree Sampler (page 102) make it a delight to stitch

USING BUTTONS AND CHARMS

buttons

I began using buttons in my work some years ago because I love the appearance of the shiny ceramic buttons against cross stitch and linen. I also like the matte flowerpot button range as they give a life-like garden effect when combined with stitched flowers. Embellishing cross stitch with a variety of buttons, charms, beads or treasures has become increasingly popular and there is now a huge range of embellishments, with most being readily available by mail order if you are unable to find them in your local needlework shop. When a particular button or charm has been used in a project in this book, its source is given in brackets in the project materials list, with details found in Suppliers on page 126.

There are now dozens of lovely buttons and charms available on a garden theme and I have used many of them in this book. As I love them so much I am always encouraging other people to make use of them too, and it is lovely to see what exciting effects can be produced.

Using Buttons

There are two main ways of incorporating a button into a cross stitch design. The first is to stitch a design completely in cross stitch and then to sew a button on top of the stitching. An example of this is the Plant Your Peas picture, where the two black crow buttons could be removed as the border is complete beneath them, so the design can still function without them (see picture detail below).

The Cottage Garden Sampler also uses a button in this way – a pretty daisy, to add to the profusion of flowers in the design.

The other way is to use a button as an integral part of the design, as in the three flowers in pots (page 14), where each button is essential to the design. The Welcome to My Garden Sampler also uses two pansy buttons and a watering can button as part of the design – to great effect (see picture detail below).

Where I have used a button as an integral part of the design, I have also charted it as a motif. This can take the place of the button if you prefer not to use it (instructions are given in the projects where this occurs).

Buttons make a design special and can really bring it to life by adding a three-dimensional quality. They are also very versatile and you can change them around if you wish, adding ones of your own choice to make your design unique. They are quick and easy to sew on, either using matching thread to blend in with the button, as I have done on the flowerpots, or with contrasting thread to add to the effect, as with the pansy buttons on the Welcome To My Garden Sampler (page 16).

Using Charms

Charms are a more subtle decorative feature but still a very attractive way of emphasising the subject matter in a design and adding interest. They are also very useful for filling a gap where most motifs would appear too large. As with buttons, charms can be used on top of cross stitch or by themselves using a matching thread. Charms are inexpensive, easy to obtain and fun to use and it is a good idea to collect them when you come across them at fairs and in needlework shops, as a selection is useful to choose from when you begin a project.

Charms

My favourite charms have always been bees, buzzing about among the stitched flowers and around beehives. A detail of the Marjoram Picture shown above illustrates the use of a bee charm to enhance a design.

Using Beads

I use beads in the same way as charms and buttons, to enhance my designs and give an extra lift and sparkle to pieces of work. You will need a beading needle to attach most beads, particularly small seed beads. I find the most secure way of anchoring a bead is by stitching a cross rather than using a single diagonal thread.

THE COTTAGE GARDEN

bright geraniums

Of all the different kinds of gardens, the cottage garden is my favourite. I love the profusion, the mixture of colours, scents, shapes and textures in a small area. There are no empty spaces and everywhere you look there is something to delight the eye, with the added visual interest of structures like beehives and pea sticks. There are climbing roses, twining honeysuckle, stately hollyhocks, cabbages nestling among flowers and pots of bright geraniums tucked into any space.

Celebrate the simple charm of the cottage garden with three lovely samplers, a collection of flowerpot buttons filled with flowers, some old-fashioned seed packets and a bookmark featuring cottage garden motifs.

THE COTTAGE GARDEN SAMPLER

The cottage garden, artless, colourful and welcoming, is reflected perfectly in this sampler, full of riotous beauty yet charming simplicity.

DESIGN SIZE: 7⅛ x 9⅝in (18 x 24.5cm)
STITCH COUNT: 101 x 136

MATERIALS

* 14 x 18in (36 x 45cm) 28 count linen in white
* DMC stranded cottons as listed in the key
* Size 26 tapestry needle
* Mill Hill daisy button (American Country Cross Stitch)
* Dragonfly charm (Heritage Stitchcraft)
* Wheelbarrow charm (Debbie Cripps)

1 Find the centre of the fabric and using an embroidery frame if you wish, begin stitching here over two fabric threads following the chart on pages 12/13. Use two strands of stranded cotton for all the stitches, except for the backstitch outlining and French

COTTAGE GARDENS

The original cottage gardens were grown from necessity rather than for the pleasure of cultivation. They contained essential things like vegetables to feed the family, herbs for medicines, hens for their eggs, beehives for honey and a few flowers to sweeten the house. Gradually though, cottage gardens became less important for subsistence living and more of a pleasure for the cottagers to enjoy and they would exchange seeds and slips with neighbours to increase their range of plants.

knots which use one strand. Stitch the daisy motif if you are not using the button.

2 When stitching is complete, sew on the button and charms with matching thread if you are using them, then press the sampler carefully and frame.

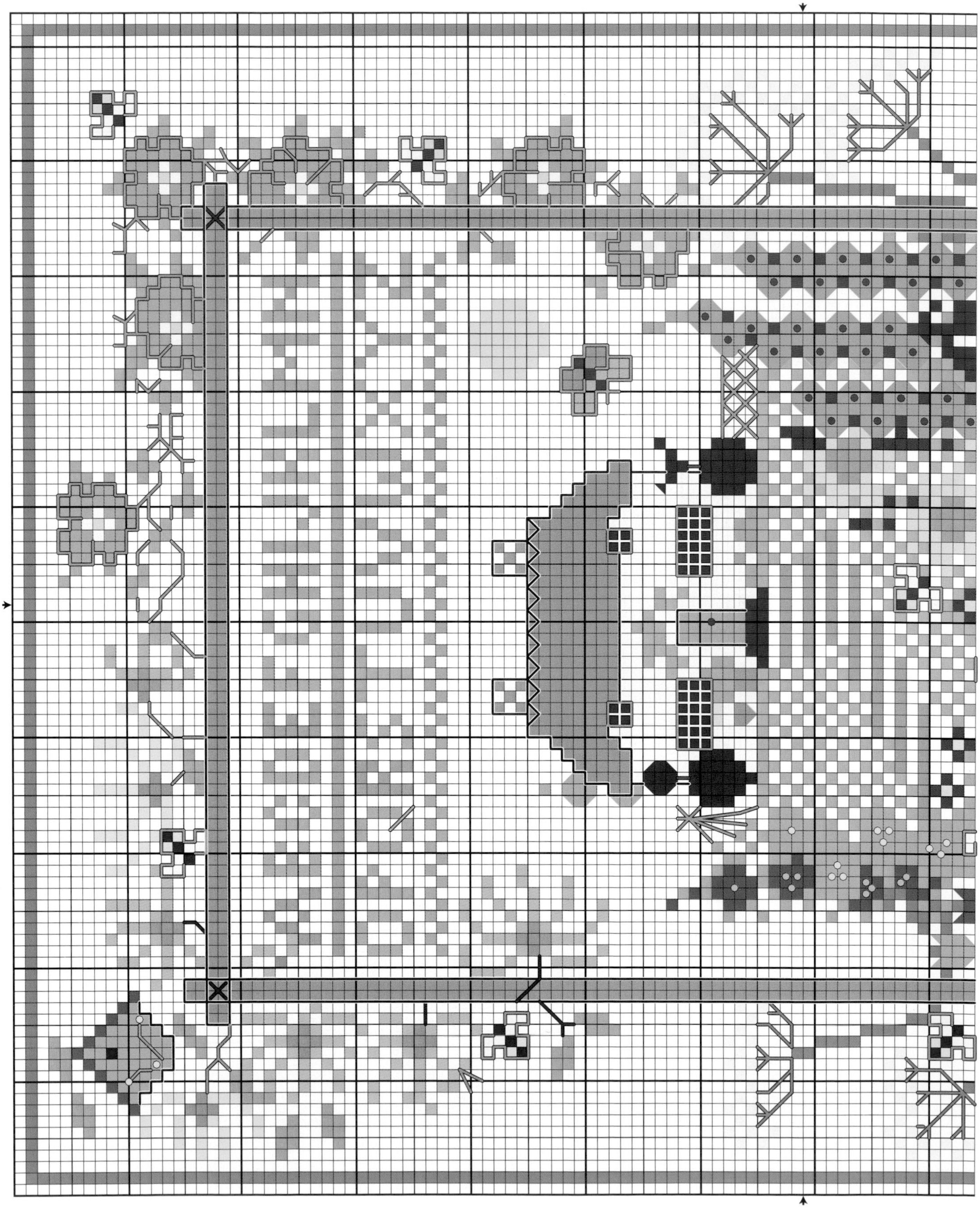

here is nowhere
more delightful than a
cottage garden on a summer
afternoon

Cottage Garden Sampler Key

DMC stranded cotton

■ 309	■ 501	□ 743
■ 340	■ 503	■ 3348
■ 352	■ 553	■ 3608
■ 413	■ 642	□ 3770
■ 436	■ 703	□ ECRU

Backstitch

— 309	— 501
— 340	— 642
— 413	— 703
— 436	— 3348
— 500	— ECRU

French knots

- ● 352
- ● 413
- ○ 743

NOTES

Stitch over two threads of white 28 count linen with DMC stranded cottons, using two strands for cross stitch and one for French knots. Backstitch outlining and lettering use one strand, but use two strands for all other backstitch. Embellishments: daisy button, dragonfly charm, wheelbarrow charm.

THREE FLOWERS IN POTS

The three designs in this set make good use of flowerpot buttons. These are great fun to design with, as adding different flowers to the various buttons produces many different effects.

Aster in White Pot

DESIGN SIZE: 1¾ x 1¾in (4.5 x 4.5cm)
STITCH COUNT: 25 x 24

MATERIALS

❀ 6 x 5in (15 x 13cm) 28 count linen in raw linen
❀ DMC stranded cottons as listed in the key
❀ Size 26 tapestry needle
❀ White flowerpot button (Debbie Cripps)

1 Find the centre of the fabric and begin stitching here over two fabric threads following the chart on page 15, using two strands of stranded cotton for the cross stitch throughout and one for the backstitch. If you are not using the flowerpot button, then stitch the motif instead using one strand of stranded cotton for the French knots and backstitch outlining.

2 When all the stitching is complete, sew on the button with matching thread, if you are using it. Make up the embroidery into a card or frame as a picture.

pretty primula

Tulip in Silver Bucket

DESIGN SIZE: 1⅛ x 2³⁄₁₆in (2.6 x 5.5cm)
STITCH COUNT: 14 x 28

MATERIALS

❀ 6 x 5in (15 x 13cm) 28 count linen in antique white
❀ DMC stranded cottons as listed in the key
❀ Size 26 tapestry needle
❀ Silver bucket button (Debbie Cripps)

1 Find the centre of the fabric and begin stitching here over two fabric threads following the chart on page 15, using two strands of stranded cotton for the cross stitch and one for the backstitch. Stitch the bucket motif if you are not using the button.

2 When all the stitching is complete, sew on the button with matching thread, if you are using it, then make up into a card or frame as a small picture.

WEATHER LORE

 Rain before seven, fine before eleven.

When the oak is before the ash, then you will only get a splash..

A dripping June sets all in tune.

Primula in Terracotta Pot

DESIGN SIZE: 1⅝ x 2½in (4 x 6.3cm)
STITCH COUNT: 23 x 36

MATERIALS

- ❀ 6 x 5in (15 x 13cm) 28 count linen in cream
- ❀ DMC stranded cottons as listed in the key
- ❀ Size 26 tapestry needle
- ❀ Terracotta flowerpot button (Debbie Cripps)

1 Find the centre of fabric and begin stitching here from the chart (right) using two strands for the cross stitch and one for the backstitch outlining. Stitch the flowerpot motif if you are not using the button.

2 When all the stitching is complete, sew on the flowerpot button with matching thread, if you are using it, then make up the embroidery into a card or frame it as a little picture.

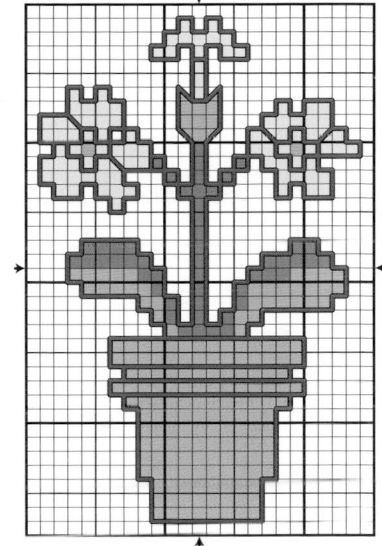

NOTES

Stitch over two threads of cream 28 count linen with DMC stranded cottons, using two strands for cross stitch and one for backstitch. Embellishments: terracotta flowerpot button.

PRIMULA IN TERRACOTTA POT KEY

DMC stranded cotton

		Backstitch
☐ 445	☐ 3609	—— 840
■ 470	■ 3827	
☐ 471		

ASTER IN WHITE POT KEY

DMC stranded cotton

		Backstitch
■ 470	☐ 744	—— 414
■ 553	· BLANC	—— 470

French knots

● 553

NOTES

Stitch over two threads of raw 28 count linen with DMC stranded cottons, using two strands for cross stitch and one for backstitch. Embellishments: white flowerpot button.

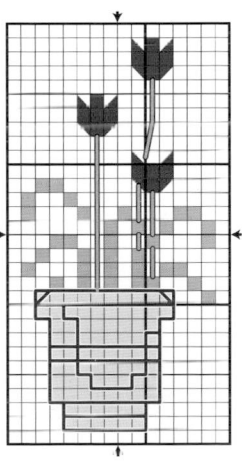

NOTES

Stitch over two threads of antique white 28 count linen with DMC stranded cottons, using two strands for cross stitch and one for backstitch. Embellishments: silver bucket button.

TULIP IN SILVER BUCKET KEY

DMC stranded cotton

		Backstitch
☐ 415	☐ 3052	—— 413
■ 915		—— 3052

WELCOME TO MY GARDEN SAMPLER

A bright and modern design, this is an exuberant and welcoming sampler to hang in your home, ideally near the door leading to your garden.

DESIGN SIZE: 6 x 8⁵/₁₆in (15.2 x 21cm)
STITCH COUNT: 85 x 117

MATERIALS

- ❀ 12 x 16in (30 x 40cm) 28 count linen in antique white
- ❀ DMC stranded cottons as listed in the key
- ❀ Size 26 tapestry needle
- ❀ Watering can button (Debbie Cripps)
- ❀ Two Mill Hill pansy buttons (American Country Cross Stitch)
- ❀ Gold flower charm (Debbie Cripps)
- ❀ Gold bee charm (Heritage Stitchcraft)

1 Find the centre of the fabric and begin stitching here over two fabric threads following the chart on pages 18/19, using two strands of stranded cotton for the cross stitch. Use one strand for the backstitch outlining and two strands of dark green 501 for the backstitch boxes framing the central motifs. This sampler uses a variegated purple thread: try to use it to create a distinctive pattern of light and dark (for example, see the lettering in the photograph). Note also that the central window box of pansies uses many three-quarter cross stitches – see page 123 for working these. If you are not intending to use the buttons, stitch the watering can motif and pansy motifs instead.

2 When all the stitching is complete, sew on the buttons and charms with matching thread if you are using them, then press your embroidery carefully and frame it.

SIGNS OF WELCOME

There are many ways to welcome people to our gardens and homes, and many of us instinctively do this, selecting attractive fencing and hedging or placing a decorative arch over the gateway. We line the pathways that lead to the house with pretty flowers, paint our front doors in bright, welcoming colours and grow sweetly scented roses and honeysuckle near the house – all to create a welcoming atmosphere and make people glad they came to visit us.

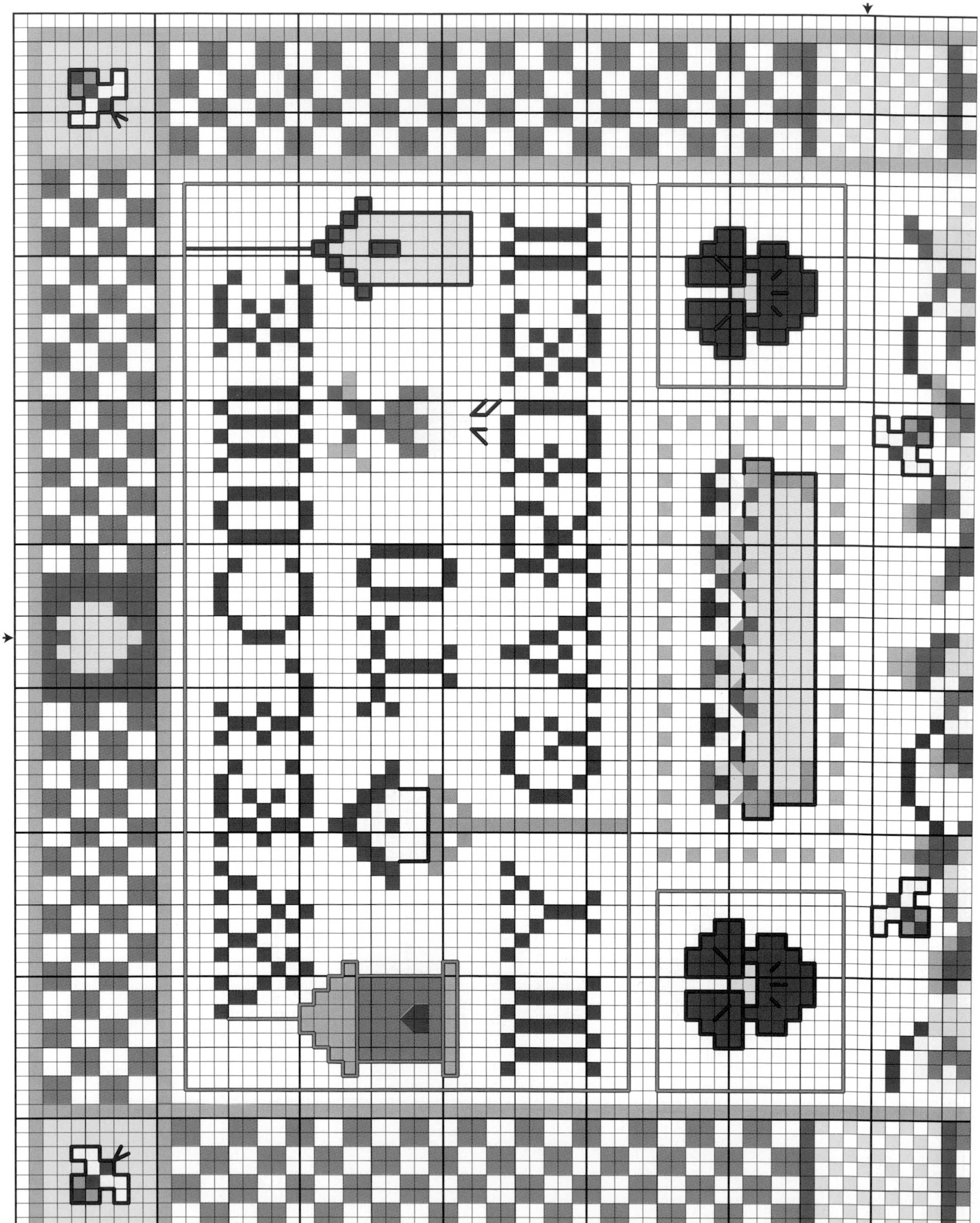

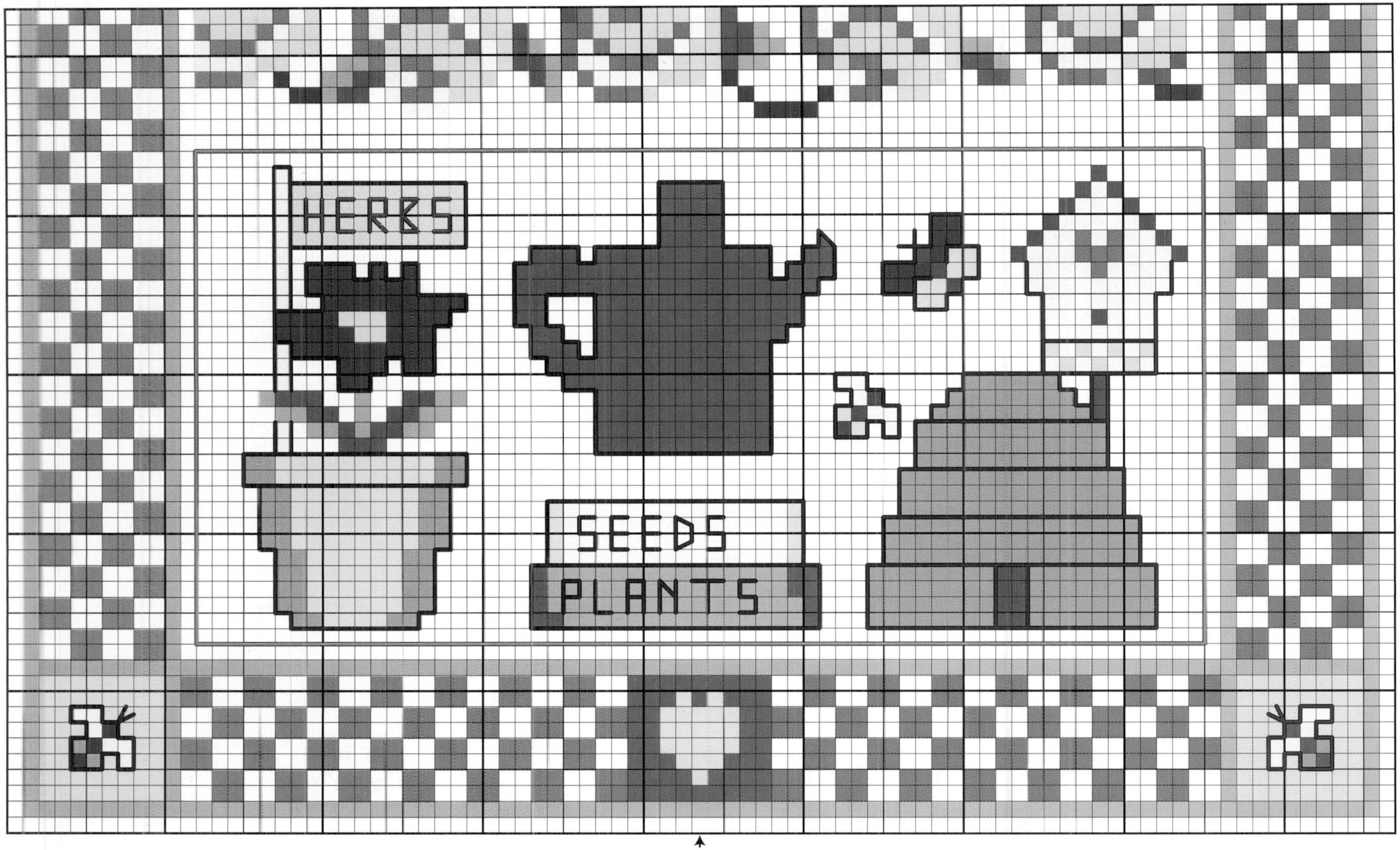

WELCOME TO MY GARDEN SAMPLER KEY

DMC stranded cotton

- ■ 317
- ■ 501
- ■ 503
- □ 676
- ■ 3045
- ■ 3607
- ■ 3609
- □ 3770
- ■ 126 VARIEGATED

Backstitch
— 317
— 501
— 126 VARIEGATED

NOTES

Stitch over two threads of antique white 28 count linen with
DMC stranded cottons, using two strands for cross stitch
and backstitch boxes and one strand for remaining backstitch.
Embellishments: watering can button, two pansy buttons,
gold flower charm, gold bee charm.

POT POURRI PICTURE

I wanted this design to capture the prettiness and variety of a pot pourri made of flower petals. The idea to use an actual pot pourri recipe as the sampler text came to me some time ago and this book seemed the perfect place for it.

rose petals

DESIGN SIZE: 5⅞ x 7⅜in (15 x 18.7cm)
STITCH COUNT: 82 x 103

MATERIALS

* 10 x 14in (25 x 35cm) 28 count linen in white
* DMC stranded cottons as listed in the key
* Size 26 tapestry needle

1 Find the centre of the fabric and begin stitching here over two threads following the chart on pages 22/23, using two strands of stranded cotton for the cross stitch and one for the backstitch and French knots.

2 When all the stitching is complete, press your work carefully and frame.

GARDEN STYLE

Cottage garden style is usually seen as a chocolate-box image of a thatched cottage, hollyhocks and roses round the door, with flowers and vegetables crowded together in profusion. And this close-planted exuberance combined with apparently artless informality seems to remain perennially popular. Many famous gardeners have used a cottage garden theme and modern garden designers too keep returning to the style, such gardens often featuring as showpieces in prestigious horticultural shows.

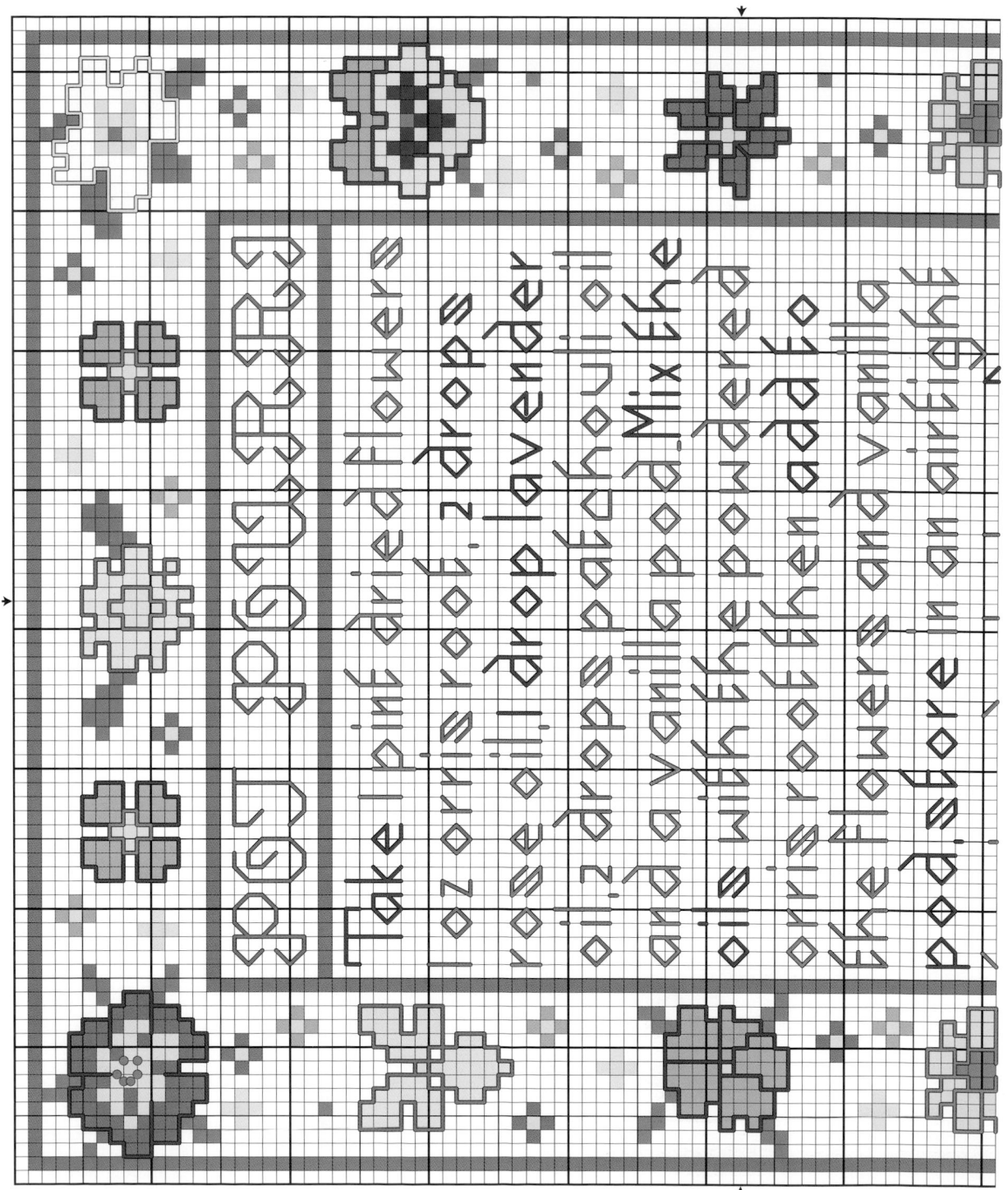

Take 1 pint dried flowers
1 oz orris root, 2 drops
rose oil, 1 drop lavender
oil, 2 drops patchouli oil
and vanilla pod. Mix the
oils with the powered
orris root then add to
the flowers and vanilla
pod. Store in an airtight

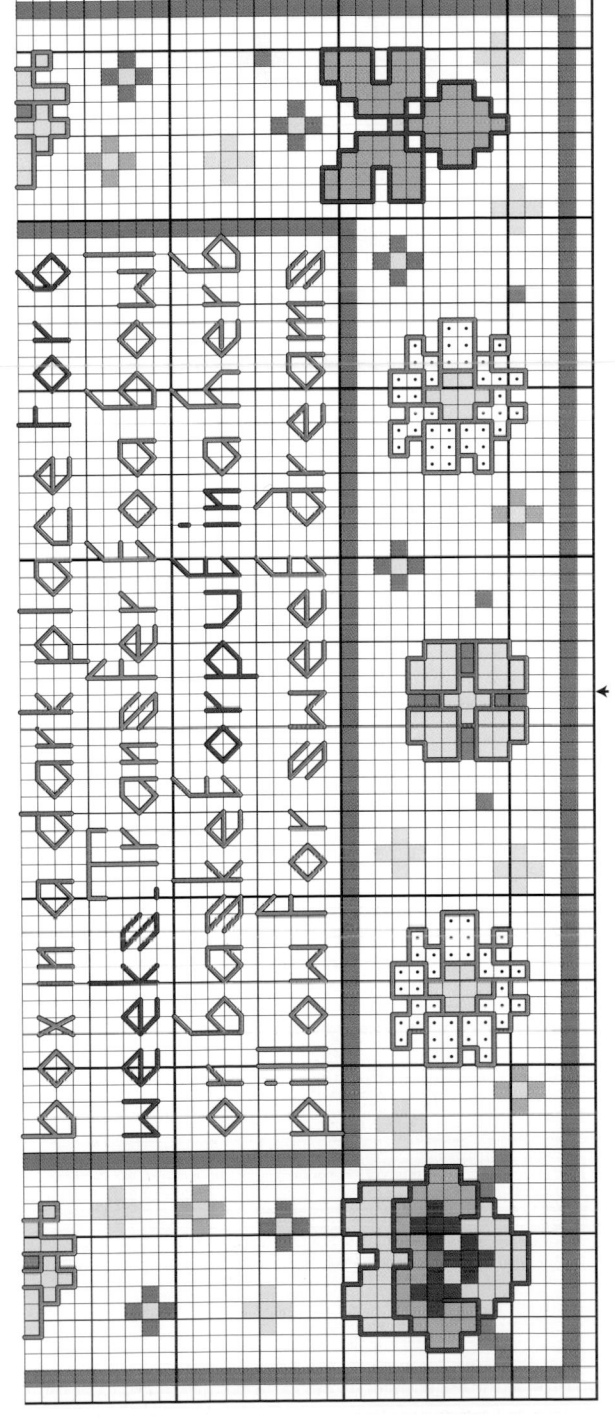

POT POURRI PICTURE KEY

DMC stranded cotton

▨ 209		▨ 3607		▨ 3608
▨ 327		▨ 3815		⊡ BLANC
▨ 340				
☐ 445				
▨ 743				

Backstitch

—— 327
—— 743
—— 3607
—— 3815

French knots

● 3815

NOTES

Stitch over two threads of white 28 count linen with DMC stranded cottons, using two strands for cross stitch and one for backstitch and French knots.

THREE FLOWER SEED PACKETS

The following three designs were inspired by old packets with their faded colours and air of nostalgia. They could be stitched as a set or you could just choose your favourite. These three designs could also feature on an apron — see page 39.

foxglove

Foxglove Seed Packet

DESIGN SIZE: 2¼ x 3⁵⁄₁₆in (5.7 x 8.3cm)
STITCH COUNT: 36 x 50

Pansy Seed Packet

DESIGN SIZE: 2¼ x 3⁵⁄₁₆in (5.7 x 8.3cm)
STITCH COUNT: 36 x 50

Auricula Seed Packet

DESIGN SIZE: 2¼ x 3⁵⁄₁₆in (5.7 x 8.4cm)
STITCH COUNT: 34 x 51

MATERIALS (FOR EACH DESIGN)

* 5 x 6in (13 x 15cm) 28 count linen in light sand
* DMC stranded cottons as listed in the key
* Size 26 tapestry needle

1 Stitch each design in the same way. Find the centre of the fabric and begin stitching here over two fabric threads following the charts on pages 24 and 25. Use two strands for the cross stitch and one for the backstitching and outlining, except for the words 'Best Seeds' which use two strands. Use one strand for the French knots.

2 When all the stitching is complete, press the embroidery and frame it.

pansy

NOTES FOR FLOWER SEED PACKETS

Stitch over two threads of light sand 28 count linen with DMC stranded cottons, using two strands for cross stitch and one for backstitch. Use two strands for 'Best Seeds'.

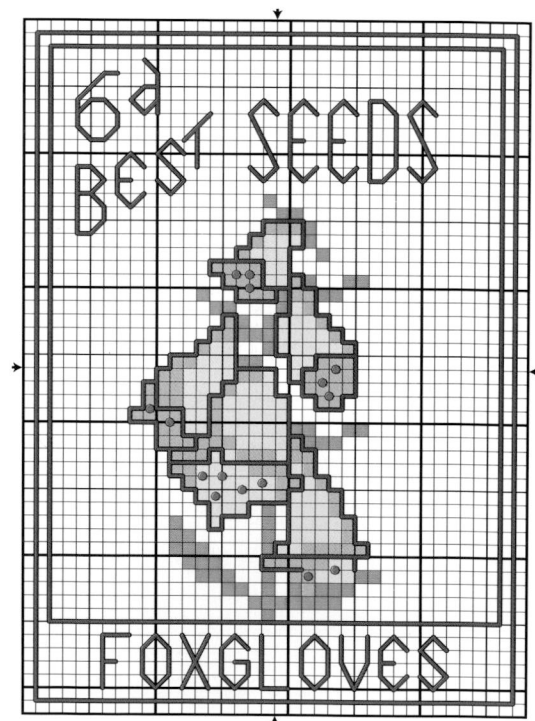

FOXGLOVE SEED PACKET KEY
DMC stranded cotton

■ 961	■ 3052	■ 3716

Backstitch ——— 840   French knots ● 3607

auricula

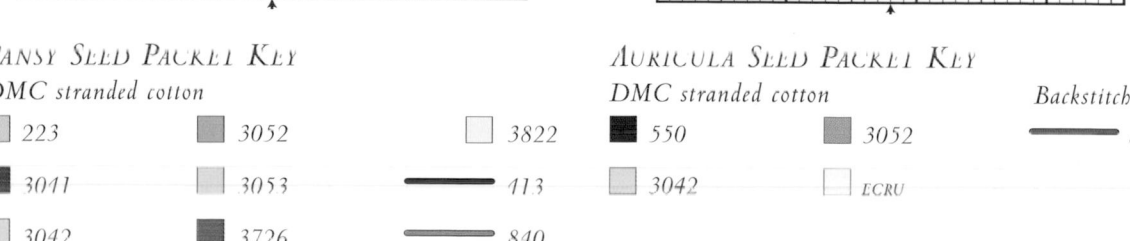

PANSY SEED PACKET KEY
DMC stranded cotton

223	3052	3822
3041	3053	———— 113
3042	3726	———— 840

AURICULA SEED PACKET KEY
DMC stranded cotton

Backstitch

550	3052	———— 840
3042	ECRU	

COTTAGE BOOKMARK

This design (see picture on page 28) was inspired by the Cottage Garden Sampler on page 10. I thought it would be interesting to stitch a cottage on stitching paper and cut it out around the solid shape of the building. I then proceeded to turn it into a bookmark, incorporating more of the garden below the cottage. This would make a lovely gift to accompany a garden book.

DESIGN SIZE: 1¾ x 7in (4.5 x 18cm)
STITCH COUNT: 22 x 92

MATERIALS

❀ Sheet of 14 count stitching paper in cream
❀ DMC stranded cottons as listed in the key
❀ Size 26 tapestry needle
❀ Gold butterfly charm (Debbie Cripps)

1 Stitch the whole design on the stitching paper first before cutting it out. Use two strands of stranded cotton for the cross stitch and one for the backstitch, working from the centre of the chart on page 28, over one hole of the stitching paper. When the stitching is complete, sew on the charm if you are using it.

2 Now cut out the bookmark carefully, one hole away from the stitching all the way round. To strengthen your bookmark you could glue a piece of card onto the back if you wish.

fragrant honeysuckle

THREE GARDEN SIGNS

These signs (see photographs on page 2 and 27) are quick to make and fun to have in kitchens, garden rooms or anywhere you keep plants in pots. They make a potted plant into an extra special present. You could easily design your own signs if you wish.

welcome to My Garden Sign

DESIGN SIZE: 2⅜ x 5½in (6 x 14cm)
STITCH COUNT: 72 x 30

MATERIALS

❀ Sheet of 14 count stitching paper in cream
❀ DMC stranded cottons as listed in the key
❀ Size 26 tapestry needle
❀ Mill Hill watering can button (American Country Cross Stitch)
❀ Sheet of thin card
❀ PVA glue
❀ Plant support stick
❀ Glue gun or impact adhesive

1 Stitch the whole design first before cutting out the shape. Work from the chart on page 29, using two strands of stranded cotton for the cross stitch and one for the backstitch over one hole of the paper. When the stitching is complete, sew on the button if you are using it.

2 With a sharp pair of pointed scissors, cut out the design shape carefully, one hole away from the stitching all round.

3 Glue thin card to the back of the design using a small amount of PVA glue. Finally, glue the stick to the centre of the back – a glue gun is ideal for this but any strong impact type glue will be suitable.

COTTAGE FLOWERS

Cottage garden flowers are easy to grow and propagate and have delightful names like granny's bonnets, love-in-a-mist and sops-in-wine. Many such flowers are annuals that bring an instant splash of colour to the garden, their lifecycle completed in one season, their seed easily collected and saved for the following year.

I Love My Garden Sign

DESIGN SIZE: 2½ x 2¾in (6.3 x 6.7cm)

STITCH COUNT: 32 x 34

MATERIALS

* Sheet of 14 count stitching paper in cream
* DMC stranded cottons as listed in the key
* Size 26 tapestry needle
* Mill Hill red heart button (American Country Cross Stitch)
* Snail and butterfly gold charms (Debbie Cripps)
* Sheet of thin card
* PVA glue
* Thin plant support stick, painted gold
* Glue gun or impact adhesive

1 Stitch the whole design before cutting it out. Work from the chart on page 29 using two strands of stranded cotton for the cross stitch over one hole. Use 3607 and 3348 in the border. When stitching is complete sew on the button and charms if using them, alternatively stitch the red heart motif from the chart.

2 With sharp, pointed scissors, cut out the design, one hole away from the stitching all round.

3 Glue a piece of thin card to the back using a small amount of PVA glue. Then attach the stick to the back using a glue gun or strong impact adhesive.

I'm in the Garden Sign

DESIGN SIZE: 10 x 1¾in (25.5 x 4.5cm)

STITCH COUNT: 131 x 22

MATERIALS

* Sheet of 14 count stitching paper in cream
* DMC stranded cottons as listed in the key
* Size 26 tapestry needle
* Two Mill Hill sunflower buttons (American Country Cross Stitch)
* Sheet of thin card
* PVA glue
* Thin wire 10in (25cm) long

1 Stitch the whole design first before cutting it out. Work from the chart on pages 28/29 using two strands of stranded cotton for the cross stitch and one for the backstitch over one hole of the paper. When all the stitching is complete, sew on the sunflower buttons if you are using them.

2 With a pair of sharp pointed scissors, cut out the design carefully, one hole away from the stitching all round.

3 Glue a piece of thin card onto the back of the embroidery using a sparing amount of PVA glue. Attach the thin wire by making two small holes, inserting the wire and twisting the ends (see photograph, page 2).

bright sunflower

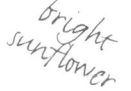

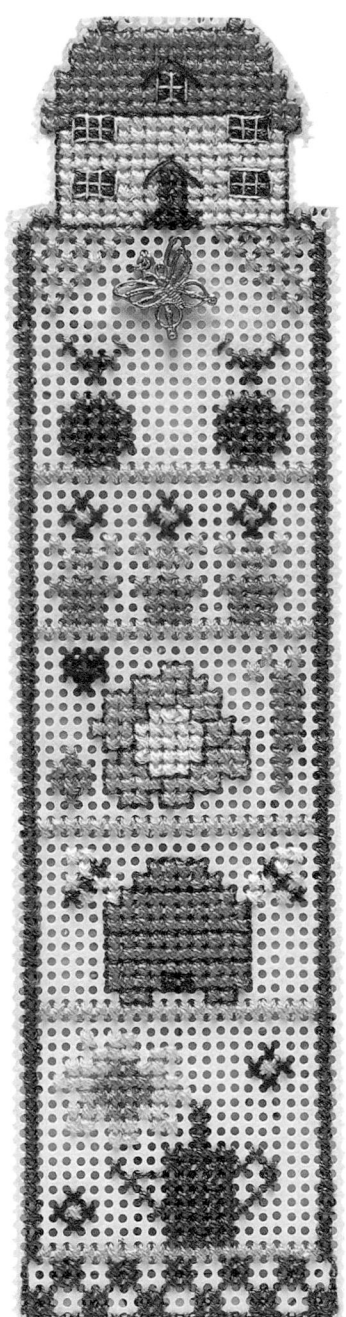

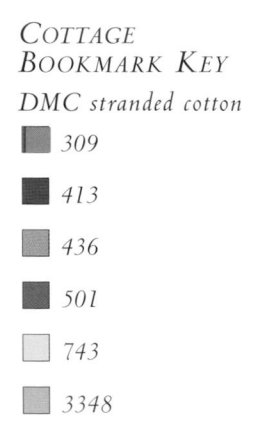

COTTAGE BOOKMARK KEY

DMC stranded cotton

■ 309

■ 413

■ 436

■ 501

□ 743

■ 3348

□ ECRU

Backstitch

──── 413

──── 501

──── ECRU

NOTES

Stitch over one hole of cream 14 count stitching paper with DMC stranded cottons, using two strands for cross stitch and one for backstitch. Use 413 back-stitch around the cottage and beehive, and 501 around the cauliflower. Embellishments: gold butterfly charm.

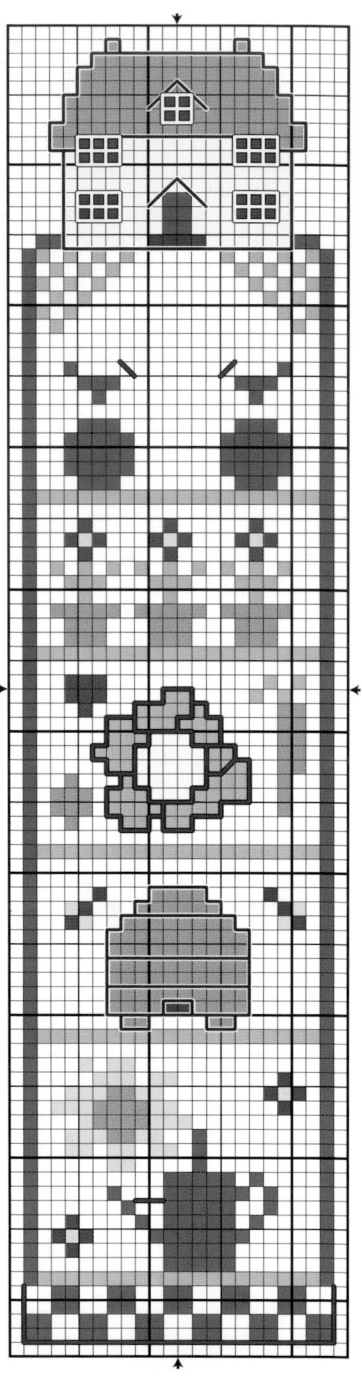

NOTES

Stitch over one hole of cream 14 count stitching paper with DMC stranded cottons, using two strands for cross stitch and one for backstitch. Embellishments: two sun-flower buttons.

I'M IN THE GARDEN SIGN KEY

DMC stranded cotton

■ 436   □• BLANC

■ 470   *Backstitch*

□ 743   ──── 839

■ 839

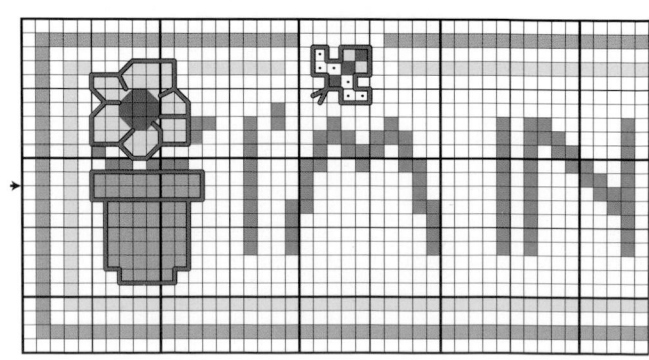

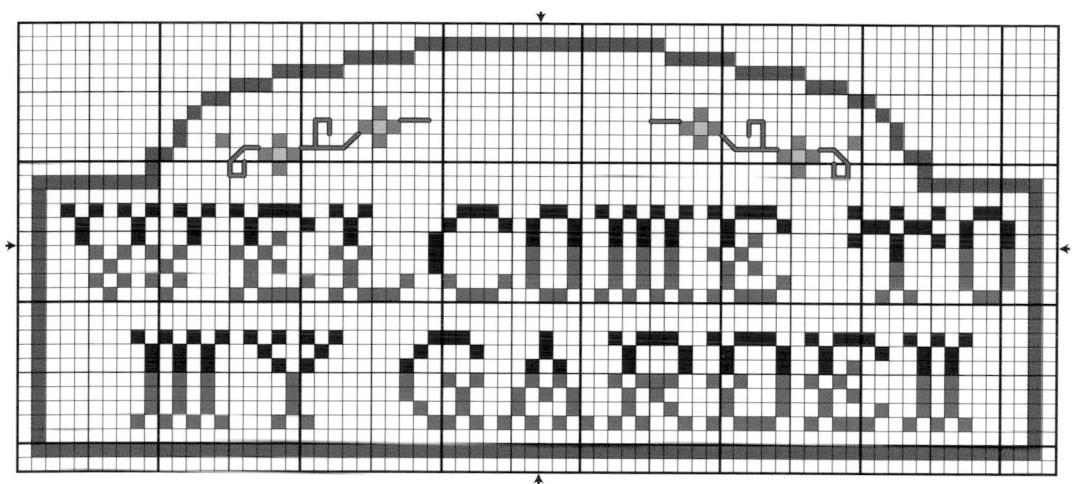

WELCOME TO MY GARDEN SIGN
KEY

DMC stranded cotton

- 309
- 312
- 500
- 501
- 3348

Backstitch

——— 501

NOTES

Stitch over one hole of cream 14 count stitching paper with DMC stranded cottons, using two strands for cross stitch and one for backstitch.
Embellishments: watering can button.

I LOVE MY GARDEN SIGN
KEY

DMC stranded cotton

- 349
- 413
- 553
- 3348
- 3607

NOTES

Stitch over one hole of cream 14 count stitching paper with DMC stranded cottons, using two strands for cross stitch and one for backstitch.
Embellishments: red heart button, gold snail charm, gold butterfly charm.

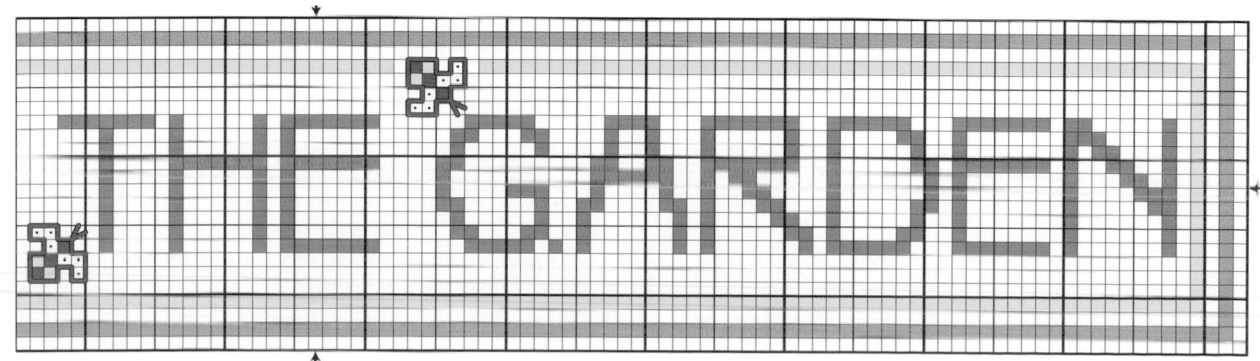

BOTANIC GARDEN SAMPLER

This sampler was inspired by early botanical books or florilegia. The depiction of a plant or flower with its name was important for identification purposes. From earliest times plants have been used for many reasons, especially medicinal, but also for pleasure. The flowers in this sampler were designed from ones I had drawn and painted, some from my own garden.

medicinal flowers

DESIGN SIZE: 6¼ x 8⅝in (16 x 21.8cm)
STITCH COUNT: 102 x 137

MATERIALS

- ❀ 12 x 16in (30 x 40cm) 28 count linen in cream
- ❀ DMC stranded cottons as listed in the key
- ❀ Size 26 tapestry needle
- ❀ Two gold butterfly charms (Debbie Cripps)
- ❀ Gold bee charm (Heritage Stitchcraft)

1 Begin stitching in the centre of the fabric following the chart on pages 32/33. Use two strands for the cross stitch and the backstitch stems. Use one strand for the backstitch lettering, the backstitch outlining and the French knots.

2 When all the stitching is complete, sew on the charms with matching thread, if you are using them. Then press your embroidery carefully and frame it.

GERARD'S HERBALL

❀ The most famous botanic herbal was compiled by John Gerard in 1597. Each plant was provided with its popular English name such as 'Mede-swete or Queene of the Medowes', a lengthy description of its appearance and 'vertues' and a botanical illustration. Gerard's writing was full of humour and interest and still makes delightful reading today. At this point in history, as men explored further and further, new plants were constantly being discovered and introduced and many feature for the first time in Gerard's Herball. It is interesting to see that many plants that were most popular in 1597 are still favourites today, despite all the subsequent new discoveries. Amongst these are daisies, daffodils, primroses, gillyflowers or carnations, pansies, lilies, marigold, lily of the valley, tulips, iris, peony, columbine, cranesbill, honeysuckle, poppies, lavender, and of course, roses. I have featured some of these flowers in my Botanic Garden Sampler. One of my own particular favourites is the daisy, whether a wild one, a cultivated marguerite, or other hybrid. Gerard suggests several uses of the daisy as a physic, including curing pain in the joints.

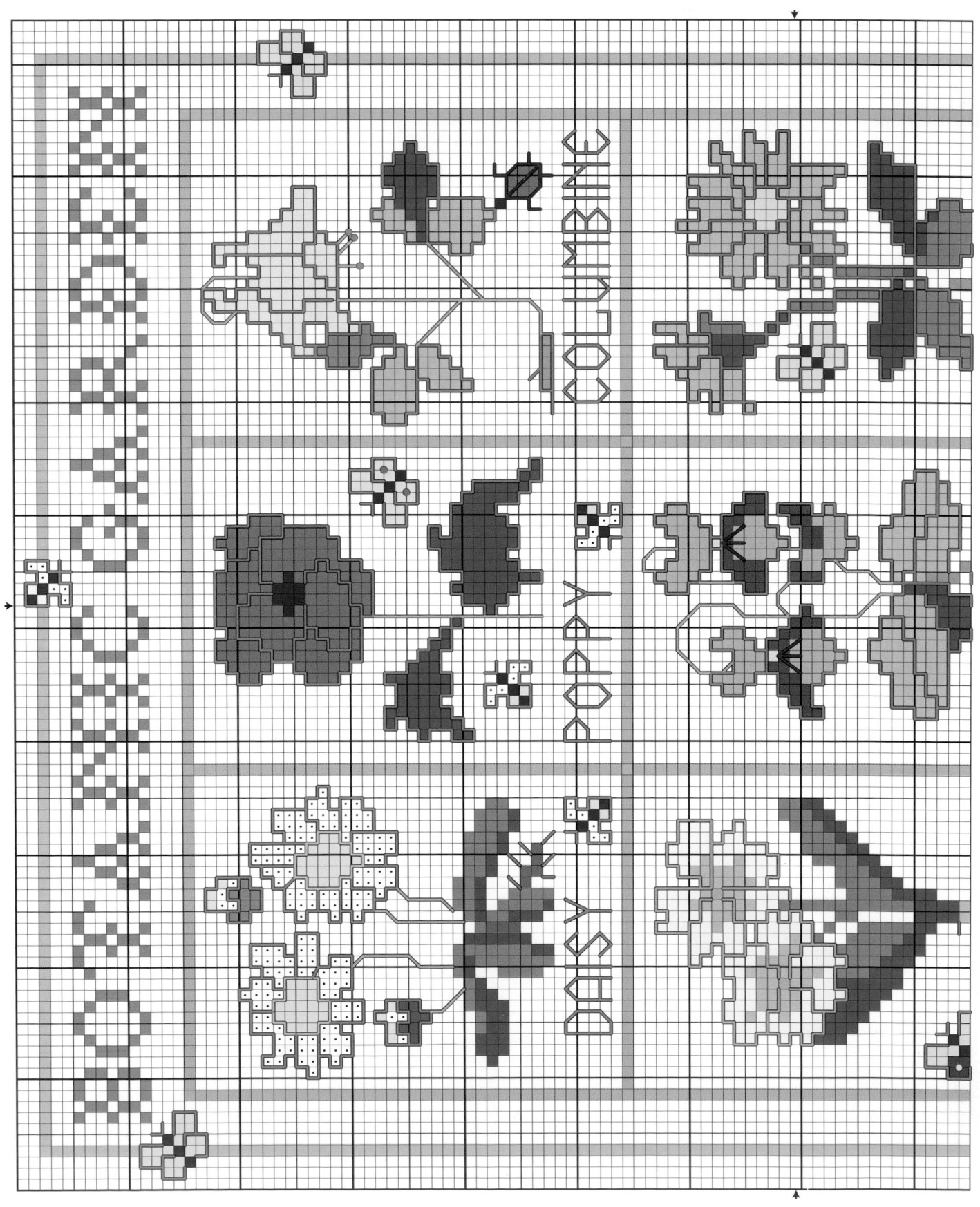

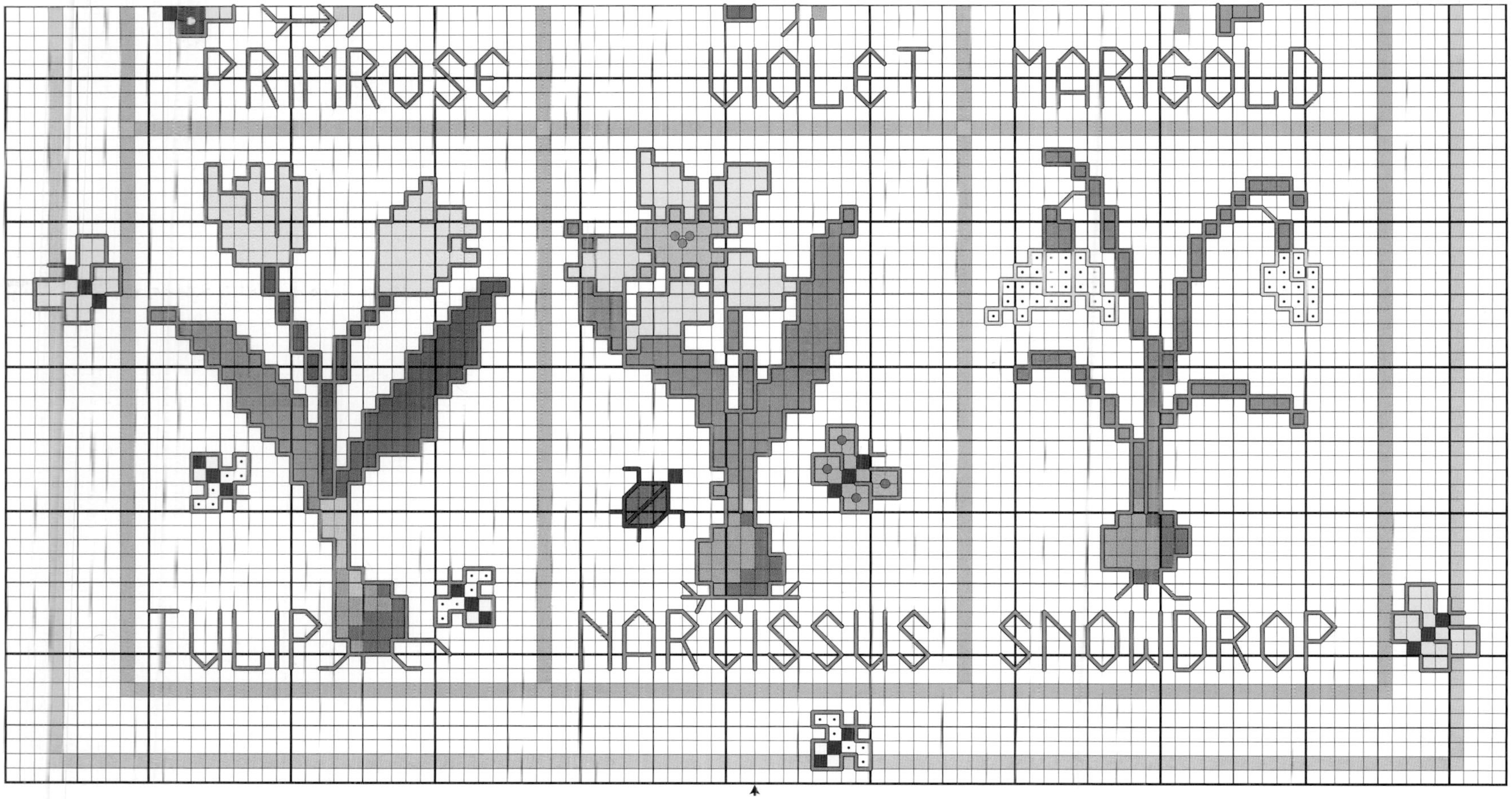

MARIGOLD

SNOWDROP

VIOLET

NARCISSUS

PRIMROSE

TULIP

Botanic Garden Sampler Key

DMC stranded cotton

340	725	3609	
413	726	3746	
420	977	3828	
470	3328	• BLANC	
471	3348		

Backstitch

——	413
——	414
——	470
——	3348

French knots

●	414
●	471
○	725
●	3328

NOTES

Stitch over two threads of cream 28 count linen with DMC stranded cottons, using two strands for cross stitch and backstitch stems and one strand for remaining backstitch and French knots. Embellishments: two gold butterfly charms, gold bee charm.

33

THE KITCHEN GARDEN

🐞🌷 *The kitchen gardens of the past hold a special sense of nostalgia for us today because they reflect a vanished world. The walled gardens, skilfully tended by gardeners' boys under the direction of the head gardener, would produce enough vegetables and fruit to feed a large household. All the techniques for growing perfect produce were handed down and the jobs were carried out in a time-consuming and labour-intensive way. Small versions of the kitchen garden such as the potager and vegetable plot were grown wherever there was space or need. Most people in the past grew some produce, even if it was only rhubarb or a few lettuces.*

The projects in this chapter reflect the many images of a kitchen garden and include a pincushion, scissors keeper, apron, samplers, pictures, cards and a bookmark.

watering can

THE KITCHEN GARDEN SAMPLER

I designed this piece as a spot sampler showing some of the many elements of this type of garden.
I chose the greens, yellows, oranges and browns to suggest vegetable colours and included a few creatures gardeners find amongst their vegetables.

DESIGN SIZE: 6 x 8in (15.2 x 20.3cm)
STITCH COUNT: 75 x 100

MATERIALS

- ❀ 14 x 18in (35 x 45cm) 28 count linen in grey
- ❀ DMC stranded cottons as listed in the key
- ❀ Size 26 tapestry needle

1 Find the centre of the fabric and begin stitching here over two threads following the chart on page 36. Use two strands for the cross stitch and one for the backstitch except for the pea tendrils which use two strands. Stitch the quotation 'Sow dry and set wet'

'I have always thought a Kitchin-garden a more pleasant sight, than the finest Orangerie, or artificial Green-house. I love to see everything in its Perfection, and am more pleased to survey my rows of Colworts and Cabbages, with a thousand nameless Pot herbs springing up in their full fragrancy and verdure, than to see the tender Plants of foreign countries.'
Joseph Addison, 'The Spectator',
6 September 1712

over one fabric thread in the space shown, using the separate chart.

2 When all the stitching is complete, press your work carefully and frame it.

A celebration of the kitchen garden in a detailed sampler and useful pincushion and scissors keeper

THE KITCHEN GARDEN SAMPLER KEY

DMC stranded cotton

- ■ 433
- ■ 434
- ■ 436
- ■ 471
- ■ 646
- ■ 840
- ■ 936
- ■ 976
- ■ 3052
- □ 3822
- ⋅ BLANC

Backstitch

- ── 433
- ── 434
- ── 471
- ── 646
- ── 840
- ── 936
- ── 3052

French knots

- ● 433
- ● 840

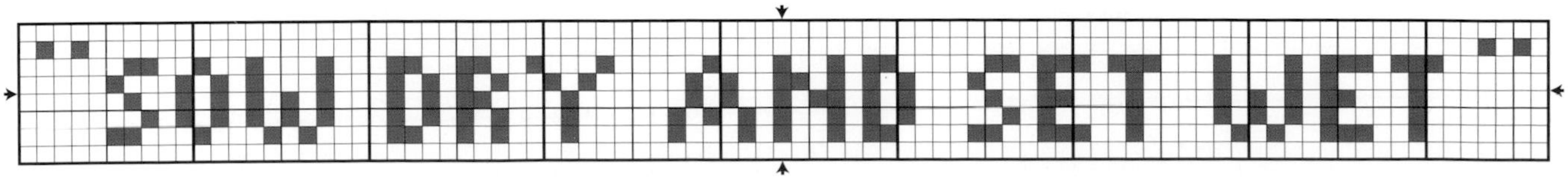

NOTES

Stitch over two threads of grey 28 count linen with DMC stranded cottons, using two strands for cross stitch, one for backstitch. Use 433 to outline the butterflies, bees, ladybird, flowerpot and seed packet. Use 840 to outline carrot and spinach labels. Use 936 to backstitch cabbage and cauliflower and outline the watering can. Use 434 to outline the peas. Use two strands of 3052 for the backstitch pea tendrils. Stitch the quotation over one thread using the separate chart.

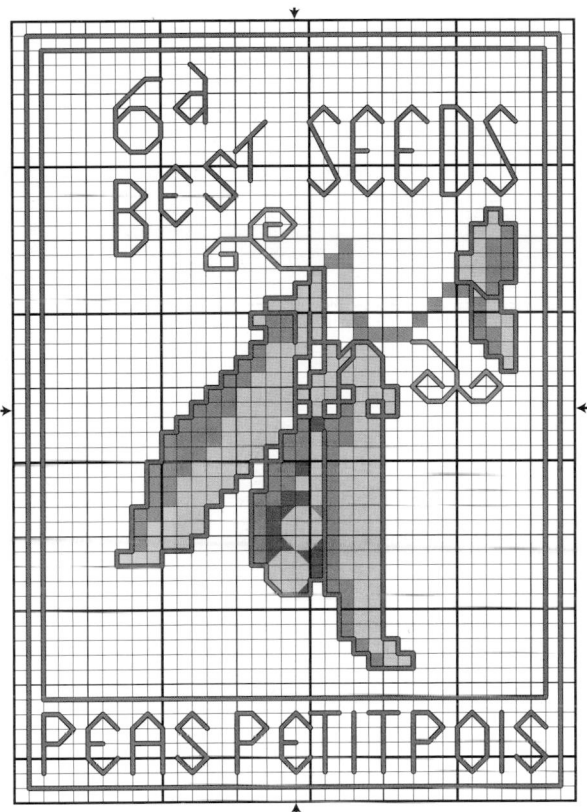

ONION
SEED PACKET
KEY

ONION
SEED PACKET
KEY

DMC stranded cotton

437

3828

3829

ECRU

Backstitch

840

PEAS SEED PACKET KEY

DMC stranded cotton

935   3052   3363

Backstitch

840   3363

NOTES FOR SEED PACKETS

Stitch over two threads of light sand 28 count linen with DMC stranded cottons, using two strands for cross stitch and one for backstitch. Use two strands for 'Best Seeds'.

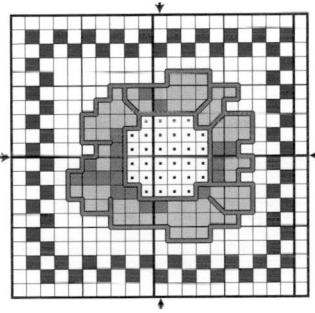

NOTES

Stitch the scissors keeper over two threads of raw 28 count linen with DMC stranded cottons, using two strands for cross stitch, one for backstitch. Embellishments: silver garden fork charm.

CAULIFLOWER SCISSORS KEEPER KEY

DMC stranded cotton

471   3345

501   BLANC

Backstitch   501

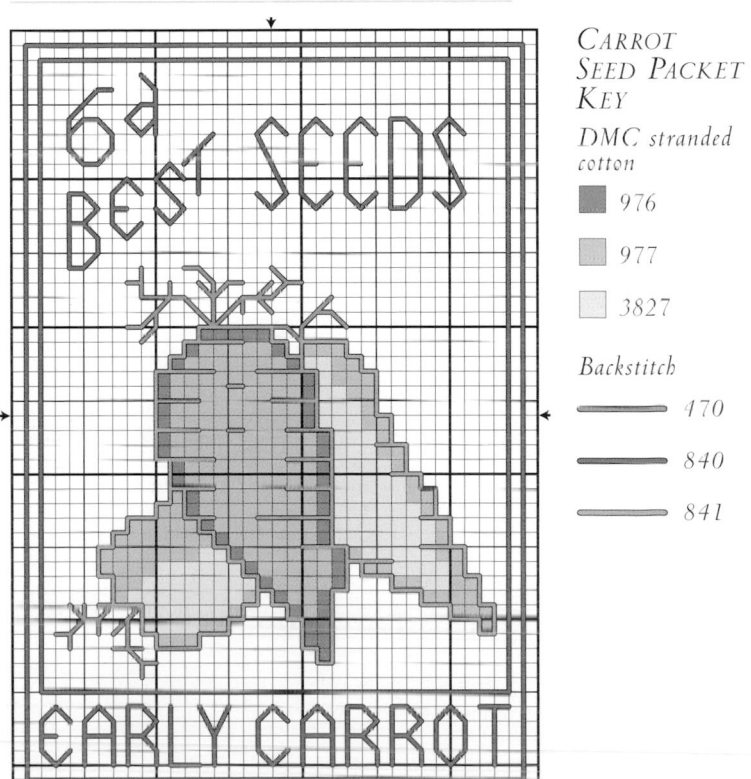

CARROT
SEED PACKET
KEY

DMC stranded cotton

976

977

3827

Backstitch

470

840

841

Potted produce

CAULIFLOWER SCISSORS KEEPER

*This small project (shown on page 35) is
an unusual departure from the flowery versions.
It accompanies the Vegetables Pincushion and
shares its rustic appearance.*

DESIGN SIZE: 1½ x 1½in (3.8 x 3.8cm)
STITCH COUNT: 19 x 18

MATERIALS

- ❀ Two 3in (7.5cm) pieces of 28 count linen
  in raw linen
- ❀ DMC stranded cottons as listed in the key
- ❀ Size 26 tapestry needle
- ❀ Silver fork charm (Debbie Cripps)
- ❀ Sewing cotton to match linen
- ❀ Small amount of polyester filling
- ❀ Length of twisted cord 16in (40cm) to match linen

1 Find the centre of one of the pieces of linen and
begin stitching over two fabric threads. Follow the
chart on page 37, using two strands of stranded
cotton for the cross stitch and one for the backstitch.

2 When the stitching is complete take the second
piece of linen and place it right sides together with the
embroidered piece. Use the sewing cotton to stitch
round three sides. Trim the seams, clip the corners and
turn right side out. Stuff firmly with polyester filling
and sew up the fourth side.

3 Make the twisted cord (see Techniques page 125)
and sew it all the way round, making a loop at the top
left-hand corner. Sew on the fork charm here with
matching cotton.

crunchy carrots

VEGETABLES PINCUSHION

*This small pincushion (see picture, page 35) was
inspired by the carrot buttons. I imagined them
growing in the plot, with other vegetables like the sweet
corn which uses French knots to create texture.*

DESIGN SIZE: 3½ x 4in (9 x 10cm)
STITCH COUNT: 49 x 56

MATERIALS

- ❀ Two pieces 7 x 8in (18 x 20cm) 28 count linen
  in raw linen
- ❀ DMC stranded cottons as listed in the key
- ❀ Size 26 tapestry needle
- ❀ Two Mill Hill carrot buttons (American
  Country Cross Stitch)
- ❀ Silver fork charm (Debbie Cripps)
- ❀ Sewing cotton to match linen
- ❀ Polyester filling
- ❀ Length of twisted cord 18in (46cm) to
  match linen

1 Find the centre of the fabric and begin stitching
here over two fabric threads following the chart on
page 42. Use two strands of stranded cotton for the
cross stitch and one for the backstitch. Use two
strands when working the French knots for the corn.

2 When all the embroidery is complete, sew on the
buttons and charm with matching thread, if you are
using them. Alternatively, stitch three more carrot
motifs from the chart in place of the buttons.

3 Make up the pincushion by placing the backing
fabric and embroidery right sides together and
stitching round three sides, using the sewing cotton.
Trim the seams, clip the corners and turn the right
way out. Stuff firmly, then sew up the fourth side.

4 Make a 18in (46cm) length of twisted cord from
thread which matches the linen (see Techniques page
125) and slipstitch this all the way round the edge of
the pincushion to finish it off.

VEGETABLE SEED PACKETS APRON

Like the flower seed packet designs in the Cottage Garden chapter, these designs were inspired by old-fashioned seed packets. This time I have applied the designs to an apron pocket (see picture, page 41), but you might choose to stitch them as a set of framed pictures instead. The instructions for applying the designs to an apron are given at the end of the embroidery instructions.

carrot Seed packet

DESIGN SIZE: 2¹/₁₆ x 3¹/₄in (5.4 x 8cm)
STITCH COUNT: 34 x 50

MATERIALS

* 5 x 6in (12.5 x 15cm) 28 count linen in light sand
* DMC stranded cottons as listed in the key
* Size 26 tapestry needle

1 Find the centre of the fabric and begin stitching here over two fabric threads following the chart on page 37. Use two strands of stranded cotton for the cross stitch and one for the backstitching and outlining, except for the words 'Best Seeds' which use two strands.

VEGETABLE GROWING TIPS

* *Harvest cabbage before frost or it will spoil.*

Plant tansy between cabbage to repel cabbage worms.

Carrots and potatoes grow best when planted during a waning moon.

Sowing wet means little to get.

peas Seed packet

DESIGN SIZE: 2³/₈ x 3¹/₄in (6 x 8cm)
STITCH COUNT: 36 x 51

MATERIALS

* 5 x 6in (12.5 x 15cm) 28 count linen in light sand
* DMC stranded cottons as listed in the key
* Size 26 tapestry needle

Stitch the design as for the Carrot Seed Packet above.

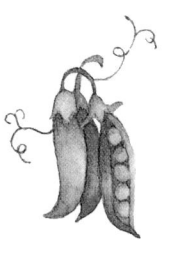

peas in a pod

Onion Seed packet

DESIGN SIZE: 2¹/₄ x 3¹/₄in (5.7 x 8cm)
STITCH COUNT: 36 x 50

MATERIALS

* 5 x 6in (12.5 x 15cm) 28 count linen in light sand
* DMC stranded cottons as listed in the key
* Size 26 tapestry needle

Stitch the design as for the Carrot Seed Packet above.

Applying the Designs to an Apron

MATERIALS

* Green apron with front pocket approximately 11in (28cm) wide x 7in (18cm) deep
* Three pieces of Bondaweb 5 x 6in (12.5 x 15cm)
* DMC stranded cotton in ecru

cabbages

1 Iron a piece of Bondaweb onto the back of each of the seed packet designs and cut the designs out so they each measure 2³/₄ x 3³/₄in (7 x 9.5cm) approximately.

2 Place the designs on the apron pocket so they have equal space all round, then iron them onto the apron fabric according to the Bondaweb instructions.

3 Sew round the edge of each design using two strands of ecru stranded cotton and blanket stitch (see page 122).

THE VEGETABLE PATCH PICTURE

*The idea for this small picture came from looking
at old gardening books, where the garden is
shown as a flat plan, often with tiny vegetables
and plants drawn on it.*

tasty and fresh

DESIGN SIZE: 2⅞ x 4⅛in (7.3 x 10.5cm)
STITCH COUNT: 40 x 57

MATERIALS

❀ 5 x 7in (12.5 x 18cm) 28 count linen in cream
❀ DMC stranded cottons as listed in the key
❀ Size 26 tapestry needle
❀ Silver wheelbarrow charm (Debbie Cripps)

1 Find the centre of the fabric and start stitching
here following the chart on page 42. Use two strands
of stranded cotton for the cross stitch and one for the
backstitch outlining. Stitch the design over two fabric
threads, except for the lettering and the two butterflies
at the top of the design which are stitched over *one*
thread using one strand. Position this part within the
grey area shown on the main chart and follow the
separate chart. Work the tops of the fence posts with
two three-quarter cross stitches, back to back.

2 When the stitching is complete sew on the charm
using matching sewing cotton, then press your
embroidery carefully and frame it.

*The delightful little Vegetable Patch Picture is featured here with
the useful Vegetable Seed Packets Apron. Elements of the picture
could be worked in a card instead, while the flower seed packet
designs on page 24 could be stitched for the apron*

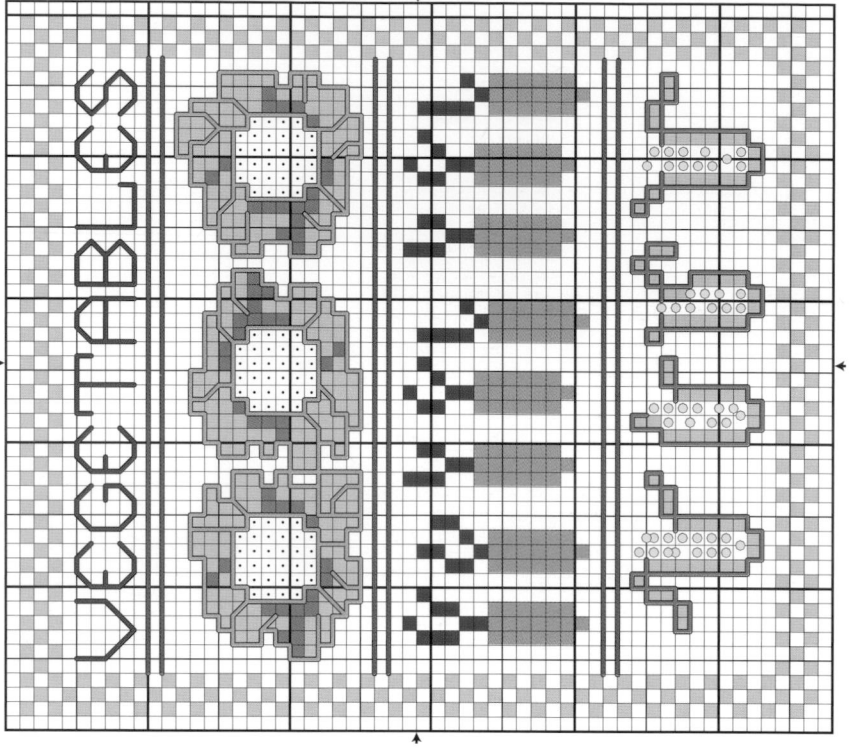

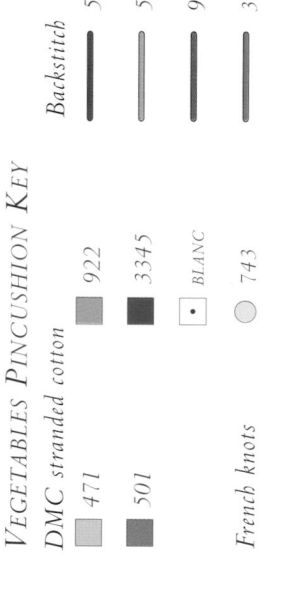

VEGETABLES PINCUSHION KEY

DMC stranded cotton

471	922	· BLANC	
501	3345		743

French knots

Backstitch

500	
501	
938	
3345	

NOTES

Stitch over two threads of raw 28 count linen with DMC stranded cottons, using two strands for cross stitch and French knots and one strand for backstitch. Embellishments: two carrot buttons, silver garden fork charm.

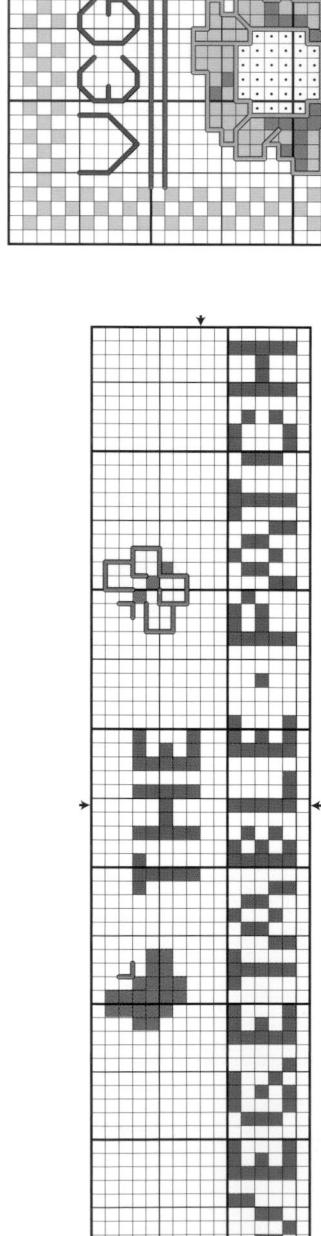

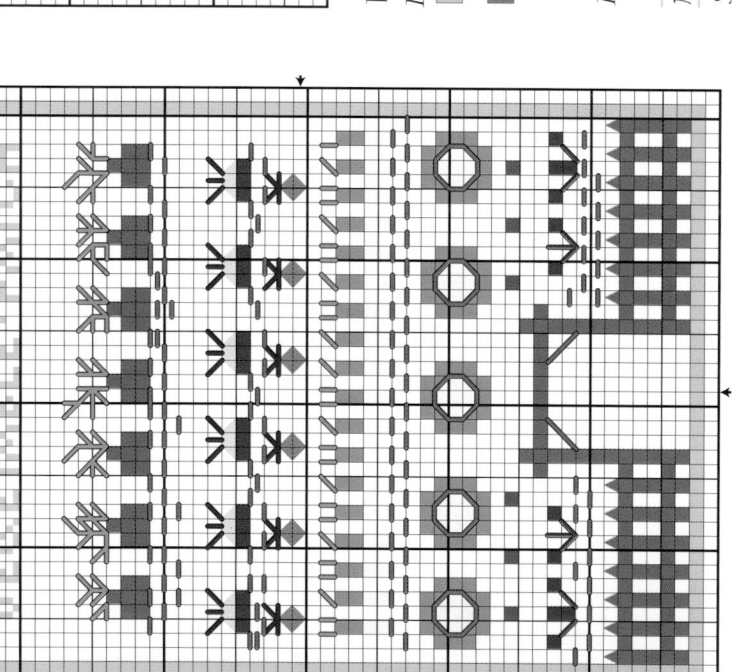

THE VEGETABLE PATCH PICTURE KEY

DMC stranded cotton

315	935
351	976
422	3609
470	ECRU
840	

Backstitch

315
470
840
935

NOTES

Stitch over two threads of cream 28 count linen with DMC stranded cottons – two strands for cross stitch, one for backstitch. Stitch lettering and butterflies over one thread using the separate chart. Embellishments: silver wheelbarrow charm.

DMC stranded
cotton

■ 310
■ 816
■ 932
■ 3362
■ 3828
□ ECRU

Backstitch

—— 310

—— 3362

NOTES

Stitch over two threads
of antique white 28
count linen with DMC
stranded cottons, using
two strands for cross
stitch and one for
backstitch.

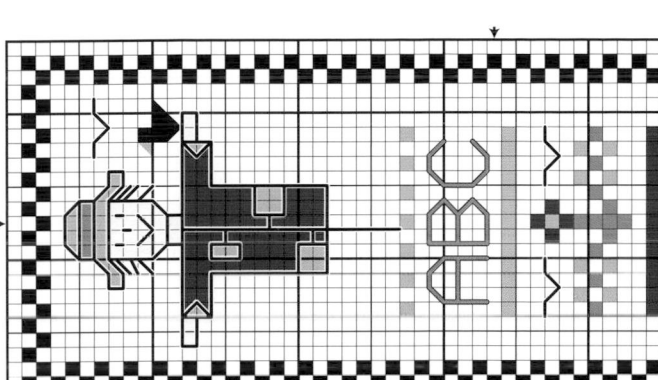

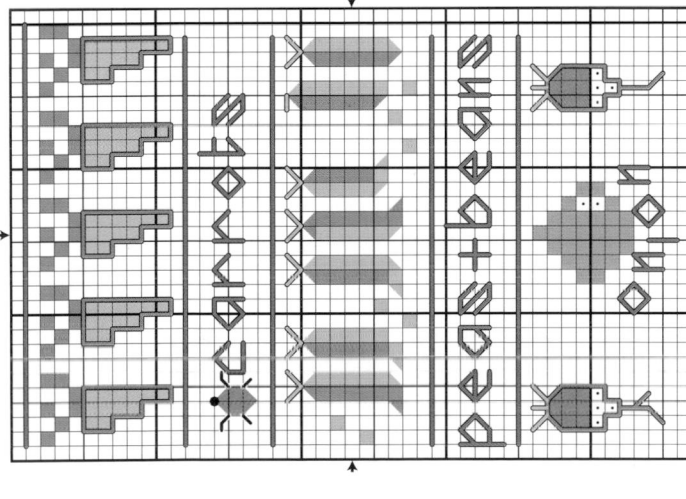

CARROTS AND PEAS CARD KEY

DMC stranded
cotton

■ 351
■ 470
■ 471
■ 977
■ 3828
· BLANC

Backstitch

—— 310
—— 471
—— 502
—— 841

French knots

● 310

NOTES

Stitch over two threads of sand 28 count linen
with DMC stranded cottons, using two strands
for cross stitch and one strand for all backstitch
and French knots.

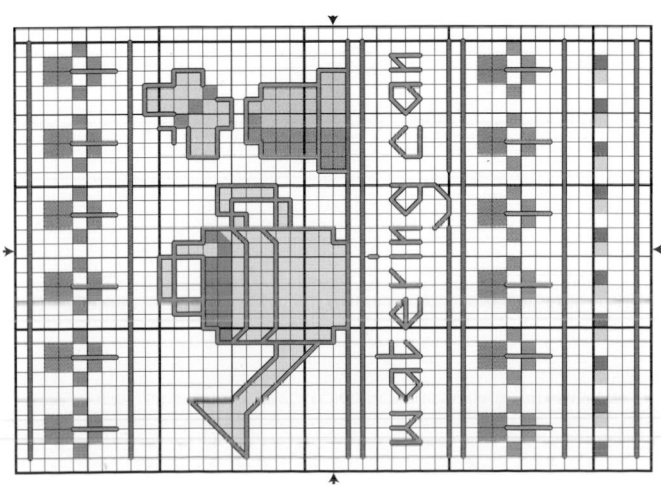

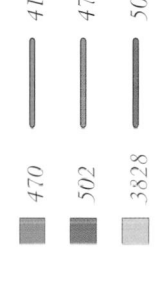

WATERING CAN CARD KEY

DMC stranded
cotton

■ 210
■ 351
■ 414
■ 415

Backstitch

—— 414
—— 470
—— 502
—— 3829

■ 470
■ 502
■ 3828
■ 3829

NOTES

Stitch over two threads of sand 28 count linen
with DMC stranded cottons, using two strands
for cross stitch and one for backstitch.

VEGETABLES CARDS

The two little cards shown opposite would be ideal to send to a gardener, especially one who grows vegetables. They could also be stitched and framed together to make small kitchen pictures or you could use stitching paper and make them into fridge magnets.

gardener's pride

carrots and peas card

DESIGN SIZE: $1\frac{7}{8}$ x $2\frac{3}{4}$in (4.8 x 7cm)
STITCH COUNT: 29 x 45

MATERIALS

* 5 x $3\frac{1}{2}$in (12.5 x 9cm) 28 count linen in sand
* DMC stranded cottons as listed in the key
* Size 26 tapestry needle
* Cream card with an aperture $2\frac{1}{4}$ x $2\frac{3}{4}$in (5.5 x 7cm)

1 Find the centre of the fabric and begin stitching here over two threads following the chart on page 43. Use two strands of stranded cotton for cross stitch and one for backstitching, outlining and French knots.

2 When the stitching is complete, press carefully and make up the card (see page 125).

PLANTING VEGETABLES

Home-grown vegetables are tasty and fresh and gardeners can choose to grow them organically if they wish. It is important to rotate crops so that the same nutrients are not taken out of the soil every year. Heavy soils should be well dug in the autumn incorporating lots of compost, and light soils should be mulched.

---

watering can card

DESIGN SIZE: $1\frac{7}{8}$ x $2\frac{5}{8}$in (4.8 x 6.5cm)
STITCH COUNT: 29 x 42

MATERIALS

* 5 x $3\frac{1}{2}$in (12.5 x 9cm) 28 count linen in sand
* DMC stranded cottons as listed in the key
* Size 26 tapestry needle
* Cream card with an aperture $2\frac{1}{4}$ x $2\frac{3}{4}$in (5.5 x 7cm)

1 Find the centre of the fabric and begin stitching here over two fabric threads following the chart on page 43. Use two strands of stranded cotton for the cross stitch and one for backstitching and outlining.

2 When the stitching is complete, press carefully and make up the card (see page 125).

SCARECROW BOOKMARK

Scarecrows aren't seen as frequently in gardens as they once were, but appear often as a folk-art image. The one shown opposite could also be made into a tiny sampler and framed with a wide card mount.

DESIGN SIZE: $1\frac{5}{8}$ x $4\frac{5}{8}$in (4.2 x 11.7cm)
STITCH COUNT: 23 x 65

MATERIALS

* 4 x 8in (10 x 20cm) 28 count linen in antique white
* DMC stranded cottons as listed in the key
* Size 26 tapestry needle
* Iron-on Vilene 2 x 5in (5 x 12.5cm)

1 Find the centre of the fabric and begin stitching here over two fabric threads following the chart on page 43, using two strands of stranded cotton for the cross stitch and one for the backstitch.

2 When the stitching is complete, press your work carefully and iron the piece of Vilene onto the back to stiffen the bookmark.

radishes

RADISHES AND RABBIT PICTURE

This simple little picture has a childlike quality and would be most attractive hung in a nursery.

DESIGN SIZE: 2¼ x 2⅞in (5.6 x 7.3cm)
STITCH COUNT: 33 x 40

MATERIALS

- 5 x 5in (12.5 x 12.5cm) 28 count linen in antique white
- DMC stranded cottons as listed in the key
- Size 26 tapestry needle

1 Find the centre of the fabric and begin stitching here over two fabric threads following the chart on page 47. Use two strands of stranded cotton for the cross stitch and one for the backstitch outlining.

2 When all the stitching is complete, press carefully and frame. (See photograph on page 45.)

PLANT YOUR PEAS PICTURE

A piece of folklore, which has several variations and appears many times in books, inspired this design (shown left). I added the two black crow buttons as they seemed appropriate, but you could stitch the picture without them.

DESIGN SIZE: 5¹⁄₁₆ x 3⅝in (13 x 9.2cm)
STITCH COUNT: 68 x 47

MATERIALS

- 8 x 7in (20 x 18cm) 28 count linen in natural
- DMC stranded cottons as listed in the key
- Size 26 tapestry needle
- Two Debbie Mumm black crow buttons (American Country Cross Stitch)

1 Find the centre of the fabric and, following the chart below, begin stitching here over two fabric threads. Use two strands for the cross stitch and one strand for the backstitch lettering and outlining.

2 When all the stitching is complete, sew on the bird buttons with matching sewing cotton, then press your embroidery carefully and frame it.

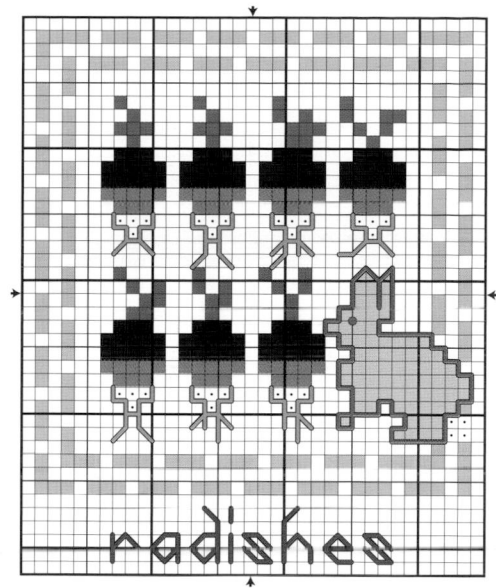

RADISHES AND RABBIT PICTURE KEY

DMC stranded cotton | | Backstitch

▓	415	▓	936	——	612
▓	612	▓	3607	——	869
▓	814	⊡	BLANC	——	936

French knots ● 936

NOTES

Stitch over two threads of antique white 28 count linen with DMC stranded cottons, using two strands for cross stitch and one for backstitch.

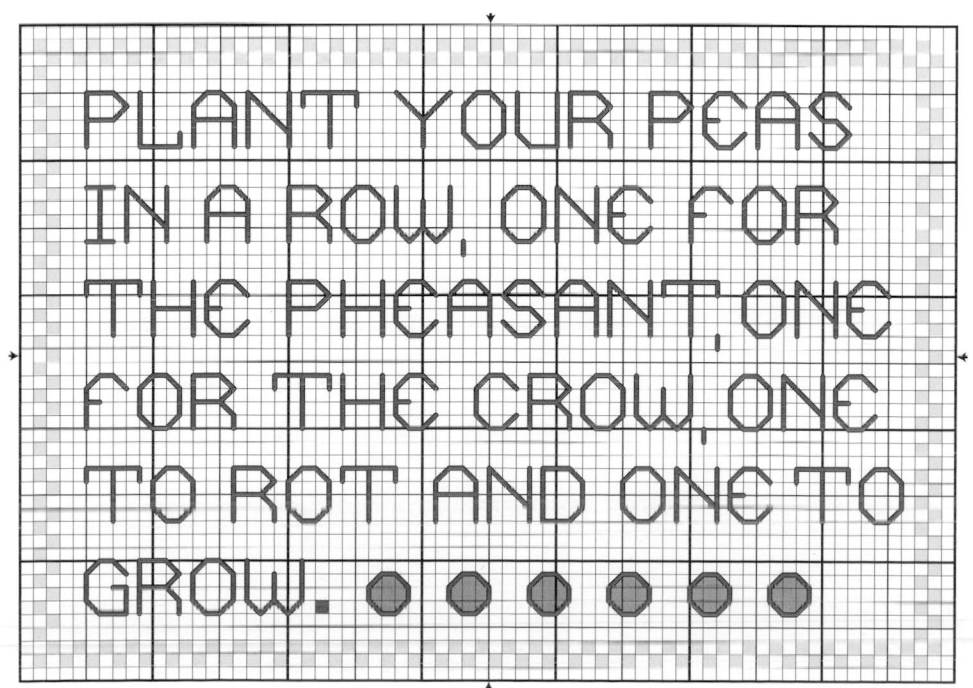

PLANT YOUR PEAS PICTURE KEY

DMC stranded cotton

▓	470
▓	500
▓	727

Backstitch
—— 500

NOTES

Stitch over two threads of natural 28 count linen with DMC stranded cottons, using two strands for cross stitch and one for backstitch.
Embellishments: two black crow buttons.

THE POTTING SHED SAMPLER

An important place in the garden, the potting shed is not always seen, but I wanted to explore the contents of this one for my garden notebook. The usual pots, tools and gardening paraphernalia are all there and even the odd spider. This sampler uses a Caron variegated thread and the best effects will be achieved by using all the variations in the thread colour.

DESIGN SIZE: 8¹¹⁄₁₆ x 11¼in (22 x 28.5cm)
STITCH COUNT: 122 x 159

MATERIALS

- ❀ 16 x 22in (40 x 56cm) 28 count linen in platinum
- ❀ DMC stranded cottons as listed in the key
- ❀ Caron Waterlilies thread 'Burnt Toast' 062
- ❀ Terracotta flowerpot button (Debbie Cripps)
- ❀ Mill Hill beehive button (American Country Cross Stitch)
- ❀ Silver fork charm (Debbie Cripps)
- ❀ Silver watering can charm (Debbie Cripps)
- ❀ Mill Hill crystal seed beads
- ❀ Beading needle

1 Find the centre of the fabric and begin stitching here over two fabric threads following the chart on pages 50/51. For the cross stitch, use two strands of stranded cotton and one strand of the Caron thread. Use one strand for the backstitching, outlining and the French knots. If you wish to add your initials, alter the backstitch letters in the bottom left-hand corner.

2 When all the stitching is complete, sew on the crystal seed beads with a beading needle and matching thread. Then sew on all the buttons and charms, if you are using them. If you prefer, you can stitch the motifs from the chart instead.

3 To finish, press your embroidery carefully and frame it.

> THE POTTING SHED
>
> No country house garden was complete without a potting shed. Here the plants were potted on and cuttings were taken. Sowing in boxes and pricking out were done ready for a new season. Shelves held seeds, fertilizers, small tools and seed catalogues as well as string, new flower pots and broken crocks. Garden tools were so well cared for they seldom needed replacing. They were kept in perfect order, cleaned well after use, oiled and rust-free in the manner expected by good head gardeners.

garden fork

THE POTTING SHED

ABCDEFG
HIJKLMN
OPQRSTU
VWXYZ

HERB

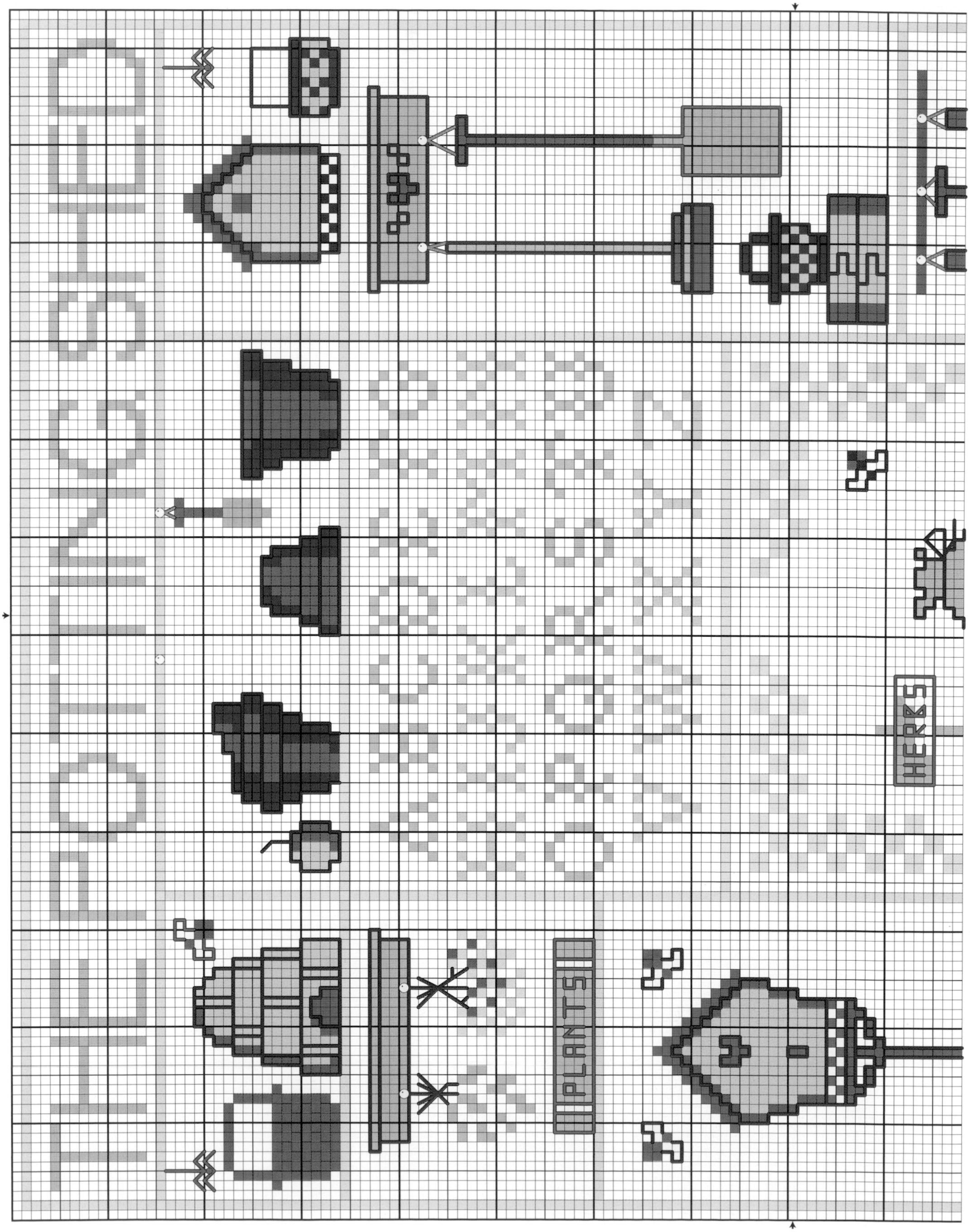

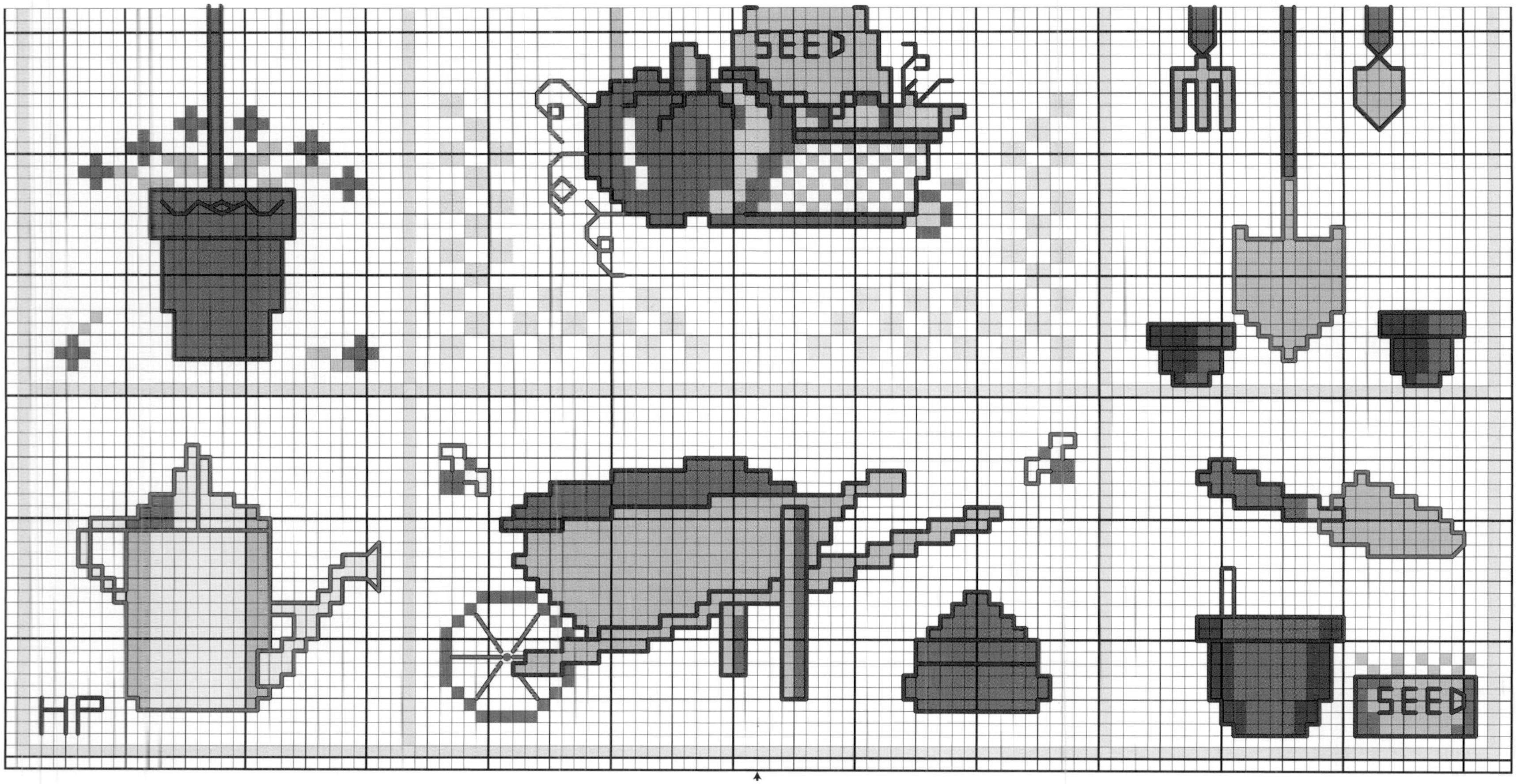

The POTTING SHED SAMPLER KEY

DMC stranded cotton

■	413
■	437
■	647
□	648
■	839

■	846
■	841
■	975
■	976

■	3053
□	ECRU
■	CARON WATERLILIES 'BURNT TOAST' 062

Backstitch

——	413
——	839
——	840
——	841

French knots

●	413

Beads

⊙	MILL HILL SILVER-LINED SEED BEADS

NOTES

Stitch over two threads of platinum 28 count linen. Use two strands of DMC stranded cotton for cross stitch and one for backstitch and French knots. Use one strand of Caron Waterlilies thread throughout.

Embellishments: terracotta flowerpot button, beehive button, silver garden fork charm, silver watering can charm, crystal seed beads.

THE FORMAL GARDEN

 The formal garden owes a great deal to architectural elements as well as to plants. Paths, pergolas, long vistas, flights of steps, yew hedges, topiary and many other structural elements form such a garden. In a sense, they are a triumph of man over nature, the ordering of wilder areas into highly elaborate plans. They look very beautiful when flowers ramble over the rigid structures, and the contrasts of solid form, colour and texture are very pleasing to the eye. Other features characteristic of the formal garden are fountains, pools, stone urns and statuary — all of which add visual interest to the scene and are well reflected in the samplers, pictures, cards and pincushion in this chapter.

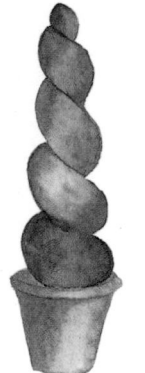

KNOT GARDEN SAMPLER

This small sampler was partly inspired by visiting several knot gardens and partly by studying old knot garden patterns in books. I decided to use the exciting DMC rayon threads because the extra shimmer of the flower colours stands out well against the dark green of the edging, resembling the effect in nature.

the art of clipping

DESIGN SIZE: 4¼ x 5⅞in (10.7 x 14.8cm)
STITCH COUNT: 59 x 82

MATERIALS

✿ 8 x 10in (20 x 25.5cm) 28 count linen in summer khaki
✿ DMC stranded cottons as listed in the key
✿ DMC rayon threads as listed in the key
✿ Size 26 tapestry needle
✿ Gold butterfly charm (Creative Beginnings)
✿ Gold dragonfly charm (Creative Beginnings)

1 Find the centre of the fabric and begin stitching here over two fabric threads following the chart on page 54. Use two strands of stranded cotton for the

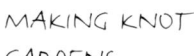

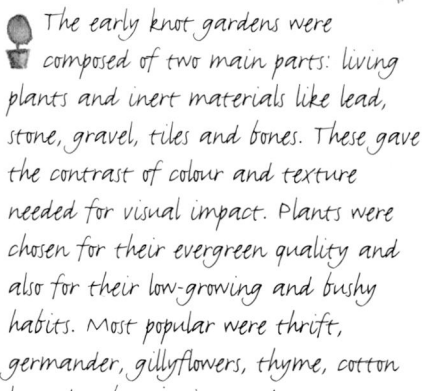

MAKING KNOT GARDENS

 The early knot gardens were composed of two main parts: living plants and inert materials like lead, stone, gravel, tiles and bones. These gave the contrast of colour and texture needed for visual impact. Plants were chosen for their evergreen quality and also for their low-growing and bushy habits. Most popular were thrift, germander, gillyflowers, thyme, cotton lavender, box, juniper and yew.

cross stitch and one for backstitching and outlining. Use only one strand of the rayon floss. Use one strand for the French knot flowers on the topiary trees.

2 When all the stitching is complete, sew on the charms with matching thread. Press your work carefully and frame to finish.

Two simple-to-stitch knot garden patterns are found in the lovely Knot Garden Sampler and Pincushion

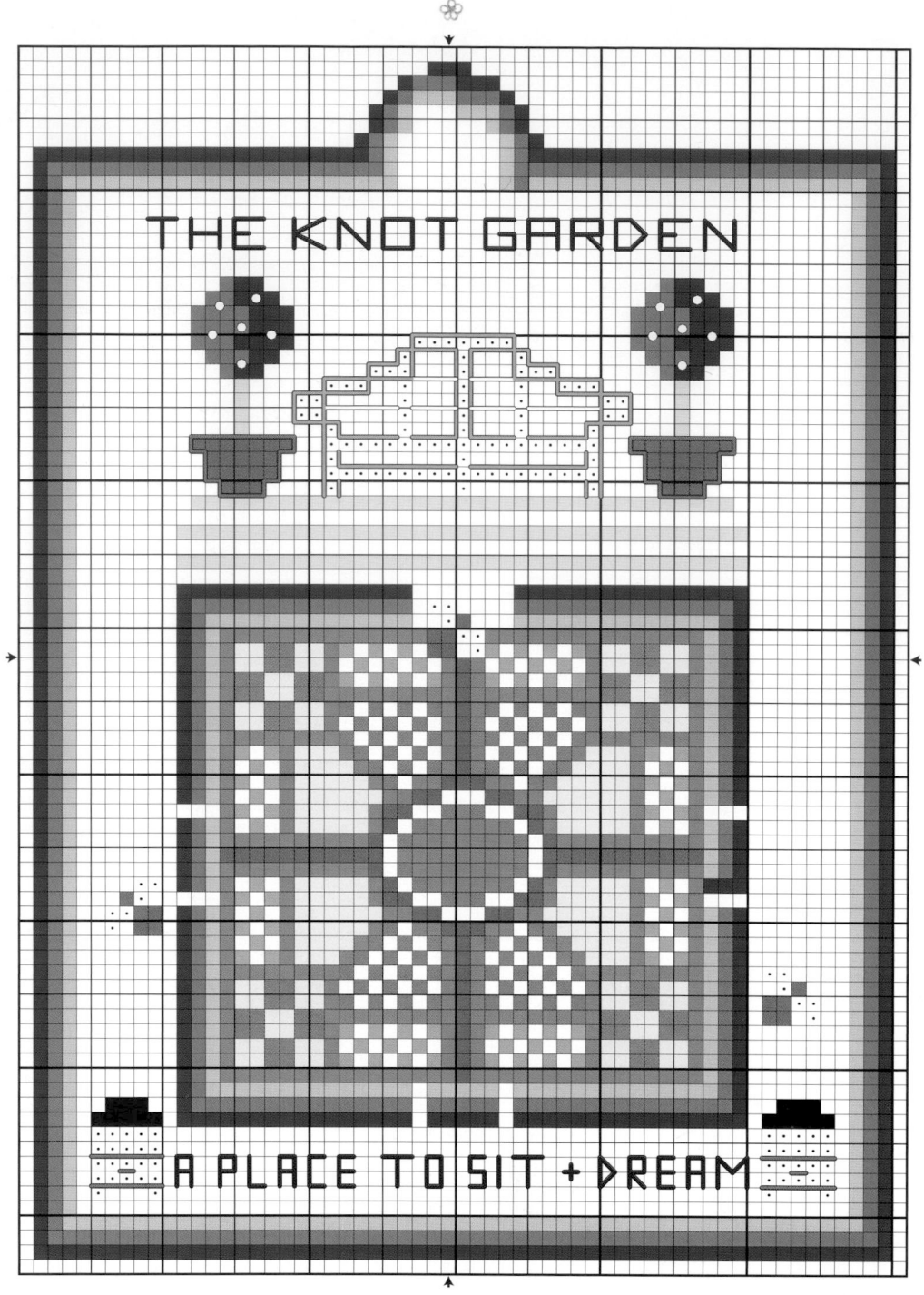

KNOT GARDEN SAMPLER KEY

DMC stranded cotton / rayon floss

■ 310	⊡ BLANC
■ 500	■ 30552 RAYON
■ 501	□ 30554 RAYON
□ 503	■ 33814 RAYON
■ 839	■ 30911 RAYON
■ 976	
□ 3023	

Backstitch

— 550
— 839
— 3023
— BLANC

French knots

○ BLANC

KNOT GARDEN PINCUSHION

This pincushion (shown on page 53) would make a lovely gift for a garden lover. It captures the pattern and subtle shading of a lavender knot garden and has a timeless charm.

DESIGN SIZE: 2⅞ x 2⅞in (7.5 x 7.5cm)
STITCH COUNT: 37 x 37

MATERIALS

❀ Two pieces 6 x 6in (15 x 15cm) 28 count linen in raw linen
❀ DMC stranded cottons as listed in the key
❀ Size 26 tapestry needle
❀ Silver sun charm (Debbie Cripps)
❀ Sewing cotton to match linen
❀ Small amount of polyester filling

1 Find the centre of one of the pieces of linen and begin stitching here over two fabric threads following the chart below, using two strands of stranded cotton for the cross stitch. When all the stitching is complete, sew on the sun charm in the centre of the design.

KNOT GARDEN DESIGN

At one time embroiderers were so highly regarded for their designing skills that they were often asked to design complex knots and parterres for gardeners to follow. The interlaced, often symmetrical, patterns with their blocks of colour created by plants or coloured gravel make wonderful patterns for needle-workers to copy and are ideal subjects for cross stitch.

2 Make up the pincushion by using the second piece of linen as a backing, placing it right sides together with the stitched piece. Using sewing cotton, sew round three sides of the pincushion, two fabric threads away from the last row of stitching. Trim the excess fabric, clip the corners and turn right side out.

3 Stuff the pincushion firmly with polyester filling and slipstitch closed the final side.

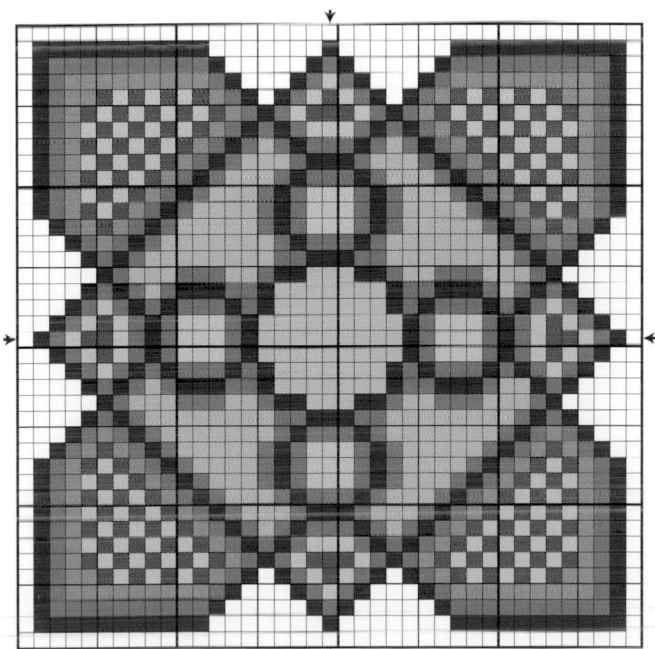

KNOT GARDEN PINCUSHION KEY
DMC stranded cotton

▇ 333	▇ 502	▇ 841
▇ 340	▇ 554	▇ 3828
▇ 500		

NOTES

Stitch over two threads of raw 28 count linen with DMC stranded cottons, using two strands for the cross stitch.
Embellishments: silver sun charm.

KNOT GARDEN PICTURE

The design for this picture (shown below) was inspired by Persian garden embroideries. The silver thread and little charm creatures give it a special feel.

DESIGN SIZE: 3¼ x 3¼in (8.3 x 8.3cm)
STITCH COUNT: 45 x 45

MATERIALS

- 6 x 6in (15 x 15cm) 28 count linen in cream
- DMC stranded cottons as listed in the key
- DMC Light Silver thread (Art. 283)
- Mill Hill purple seed beads (No.00252)
- Beading needle
- Four gold insect charms (Creative Beginnings)

1 Find the centre of the fabric and begin stitching here over two fabric threads following the chart opposite. Use two strands of stranded cotton for the cross stitch and one strand of the silver thread.

2 When all the stitching is complete, sew on the insect charms and the four seed beads using the beading needle. Then press your work carefully and frame.

garden shears

WEEDING

Gravel paths are best raked before weeding to loosen the weeds. An old kitchen knife is also a useful tool for removing weeds, especially between paving stones.

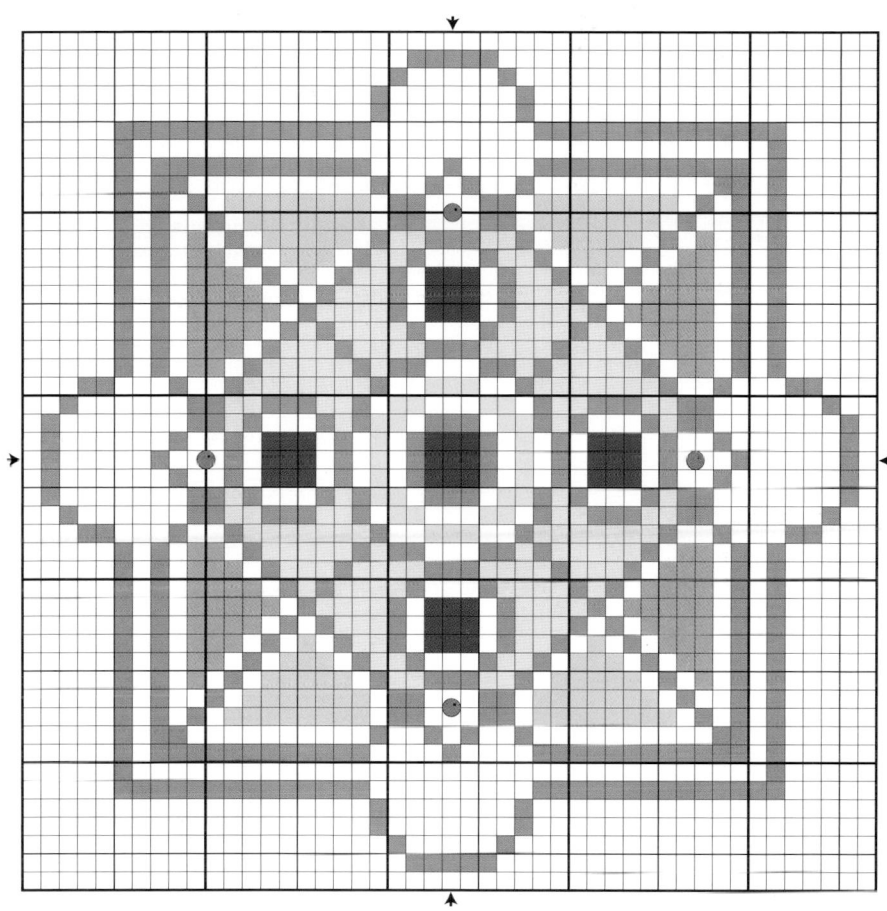

CARING FOR KNOT GARDENS

Knot gardens needed a great deal of care and maintenance. A supply of replacement plants would be grown ready to plant in the place of any lost in the winter frosts and snows. The bushy plants which formed the edging had to be well-trimmed at all times or the shape would be lost, and no plant could be allowed to grow too large and dominate the area in which it grew. No weeds could be allowed to mar the effect either. Summer drought meant careful and regular watering, and also at this time of year the removal of snails and other pests.

KNOT GARDEN PICTURE KEY

DMC stranded cotton

 333

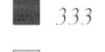 341

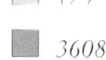 471

725

3608

LIGHT SILVER THREAD (ART 283)

Beads

 MILL HILL PURPLE SEED BEADS

NOTES

Stitch over two threads of cream 28 count linen with DMC stranded cottons, using two strands for cross stitch and one for backstitch. Use one strand of the silver thread throughout. Embellishments: four gold insect charms, purple seed beads.

TOPIARY SAMPLER

I love topiary in all its forms, from the classical to the whimsical and have often included topiary trees in my designs. This sampler has a romantic feel and was inspired by visiting a garden in Kent, filled with lavender, topiary and places to sit and enjoy them.

DESIGN SIZE: 5¼ x 9¼in (13.2 x 23.5cm)
STITCH COUNT: 75 x 131

MATERIALS

* 10 x 13in (25.5 x 33cm) 28 count linen in antique white
* DMC stranded cottons as listed in the key
* Caron Waterlilies thread 'Hyacinth' 110
* Size 26 tapestry needle
* Mill Hill cream heart treasure (American Country Cross Stitch)
* Two flowerpot buttons (Debbie Cripps)

1 Find the centre of the fabric and begin stitching here over two fabric threads following the chart on page 62. Use two strands for the cross stitch, two strands for the outer backstitch border and one strand for the rest of the backstitching and all the Caron

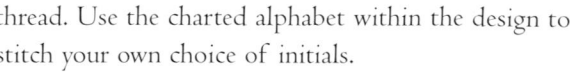

TOPIARY CREATIONS

In 1618 topiary was highly regarded as an attractive and imaginative garden element, as this contemporary quotation from William Lawson's book 'A New Orchard and Garden' shows:

'Your Gardiner can frame your lesser wood to the shape of men armed in the field, ready to give battell; or swift running Grey hounds; or of well sented and true running Hounds, to chase the Deere, or hunt the Hare. This kind of hunting shall not waste your corne, nor much your coyne.'

thread. Use the charted alphabet within the design to stitch your own choice of initials.

2 When stitching is complete, sew on the heart treasure and the flowerpot buttons with matching thread, if you are using them. Alternatively, stitch the motifs from the chart.

3 Once complete, press your embroidery carefully and frame it.

fanciful shapes

TOPIARY TREES IN POTS PICTURE

Designed to show a range of different forms of topiary and using the various flowerpot buttons, this design is quick and fun to stitch.

DESIGN SIZE: $6\frac{5}{8}$ x $2\frac{3}{4}$in (17 x 7cm)
STITCH COUNT: 91 x 40

MATERIALS

❀ 11 x 6in (28 x 15cm) 28 count linen in sand
❀ DMC stranded cottons as listed in the key
❀ Size 26 tapestry needle
❀ Five terracotta flowerpot buttons (Debbie Cripps)

1 Find the centre of the fabric and begin stitching here over two fabric threads following the chart on page 63, using two strands of stranded cotton for all the stitching.

2 When the stitching is complete sew on the flowerpot buttons with matching thread at the base of each tree (see photograph above). If you are not using the buttons, then stitch the flowerpot motifs from the chart instead.

3 Once complete, press the finished work carefully, avoiding the buttons, and frame it.

TOPIARY TREE SACHET

This dainty sachet (shown opposite) echoes the pastel colours of the Topiary Sampler and the little topiary tree in its white pot is very pretty. You could use it to contain a gift of soap or perfume or make it into a scented sachet by filling it with pot pourri or lavender. Alternatively, the design could be made up into a card.

DESIGN SIZE: 1 x $2\frac{1}{2}$in (2.5 x 6.3cm)
STITCH COUNT: 16 x 38

MATERIALS

❀ Two 5 x $4\frac{1}{4}$in (12.5 x 11cm) pieces of 28 count linen in cream
❀ DMC stranded cottons as listed in the key
❀ Caron Waterlilies thread 'Hyacinth' 110
❀ Two tiny silver heart charms (Debbie Cripps)
❀ Sewing cotton to match linen
❀ 8in (20cm) narrow lilac ribbon

1 Find the centre of one of the pieces of fabric and begin stitching here over two fabric threads following the chart on page 63. Use two strands for the cross stitch and one strand for the Caron thread and backstitch outlining. When all the stitching is complete, sew on the charms (see photograph for positions).

2 To make up the bag, use matching sewing cotton to turn a small hem at the top of both the front and

TOPIARY TREES

Fertilise topiary trees in pots once a year. Remove weeds from the pot and add a new layer of fresh soil or compost to the top of the pot – called a top dressing. Topiary trees are best clipped regularly to retain their shapes and make sure they are watered during dry spells. Clippings can be used for cuttings for more plants.

TOPIARY TREE CARD

This simple but stylish little design is extremely quick to stitch and would be ideal for many occasions.

DESIGN SIZE: 2⅜ x 2½in (6 x 6.3cm)
STITCH COUNT: 34 x 36

MATERIALS

❀ 4 x 4in (10 x 10cm) 28 count linen in cream
❀ DMC stranded cottons as listed in the key
❀ Size 26 tapestry needle
❀ Cream card with 2¾ x 2¾in aperture

back pieces of linen. Two rows from each hem, withdraw three threads for the ribbon row. Place the linen pieces right sides together and sew up the bottom and sides of the bag. Trim the seams, clip the corners and press.

3 Turn the bag through to the right side, thread the ribbon through and pull up.

1 Stitch over two threads using two strands for cross stitch, one for backstitch, following the chart on page 63.

2 When all the stitching is complete, make the embroidery up into a card (see page 125).

The Topiary Tree Sachet could be made up into a pretty card, while the Topiary Tree Card could be a pincushion

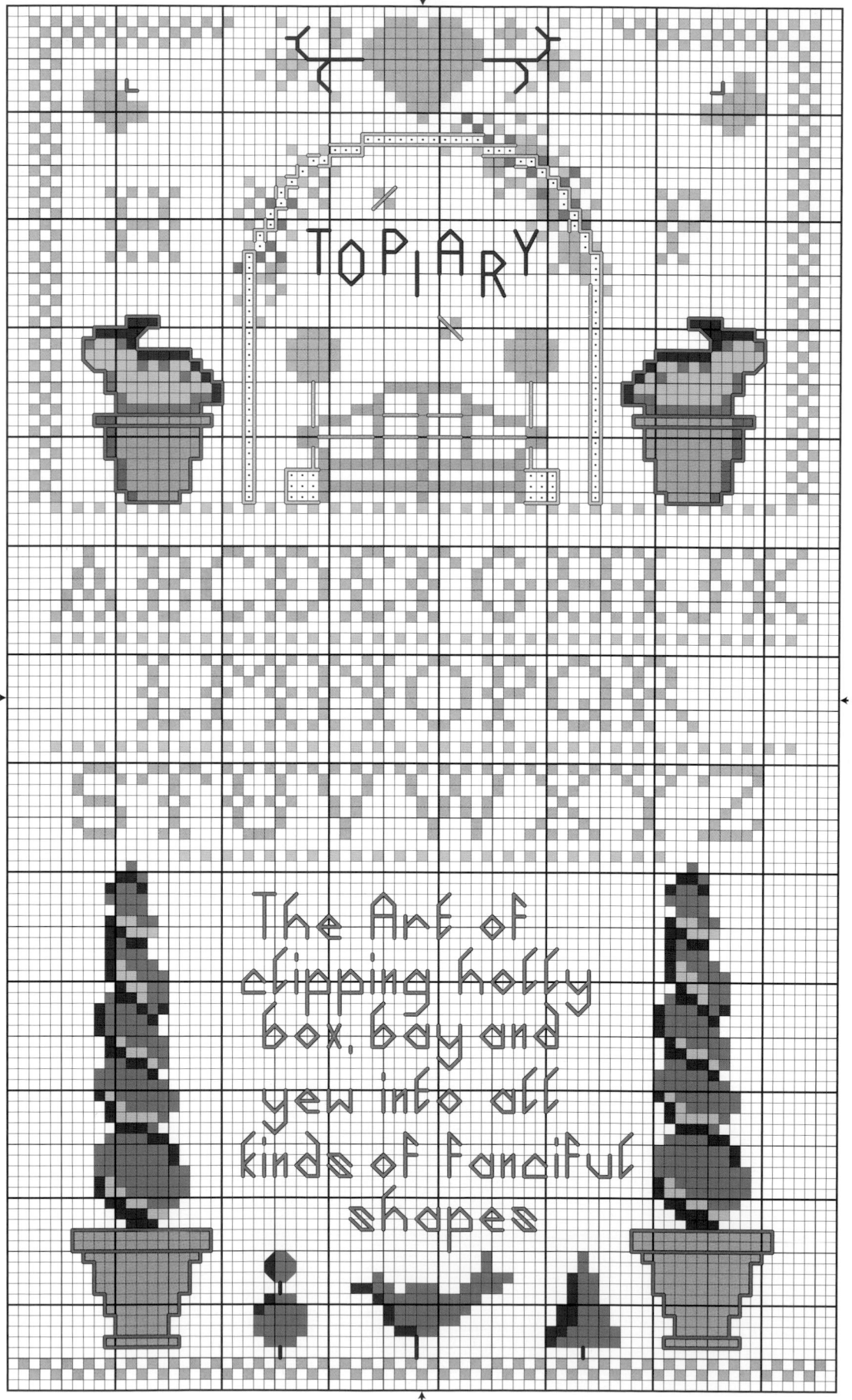

TOPIARY

The Art of clipping holly box, bay and yew into all kinds of fanciful shapes

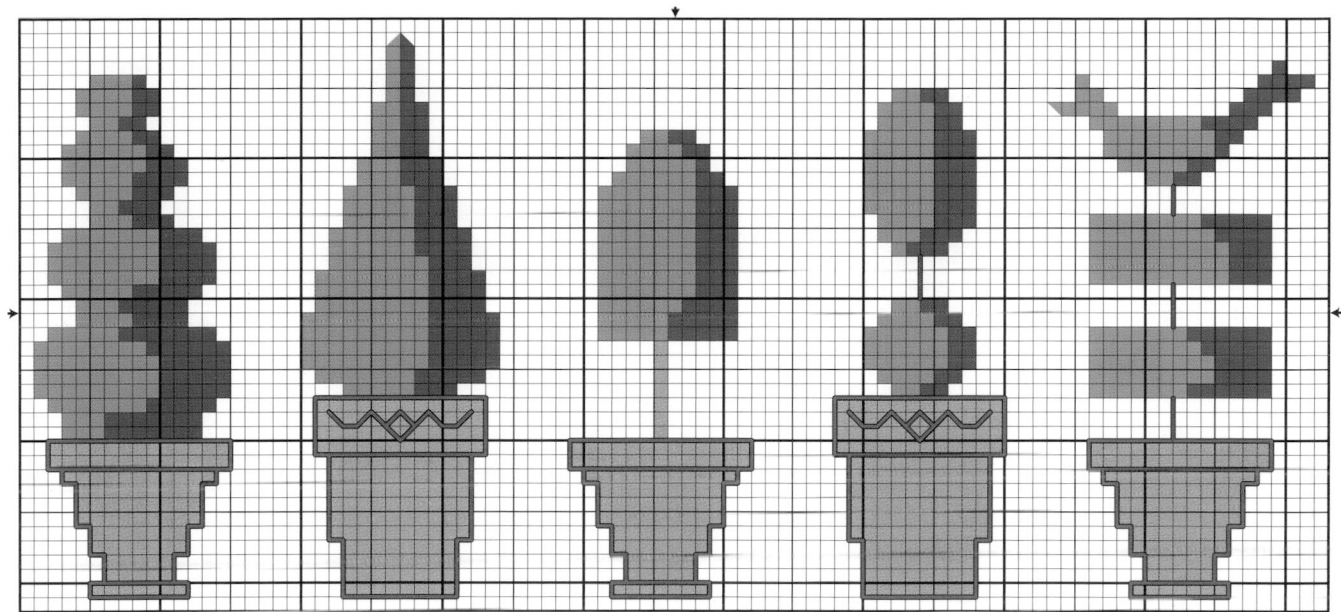

TOPIARY TREES IN POTS PICTURE KEY

DMC stranded cotton

■ 436   ■ 500   ■ 501

Backstitch ———— 317   ———— 501

NOTES

Stitch over two threads of sand 28 count linen using two strands of DMC stranded cottons throughout.
Embellishments: five terracotta flowerpot buttons.

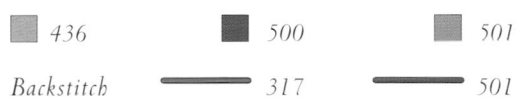

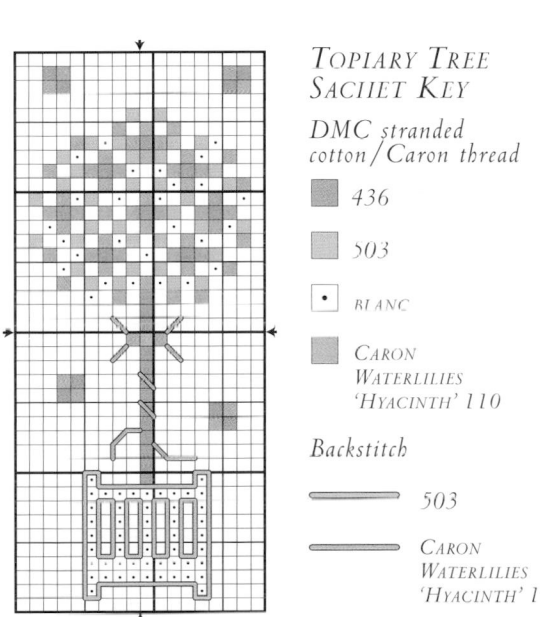

TOPIARY TREE SACHET KEY

DMC stranded cotton / Caron thread

■ 436

■ 503

· BLANC

■ CARON
WATERLILIES
'HYACINTH' 110

Backstitch

———— 503

———— CARON
WATERLILIES
'HYACINTH' 110

NOTES

Stitch over two threads of cream 28 count linen with DMC stranded cottons, using two strands for cross stitch and one strand for backstitch and the Caron thread.
Embellishments: two silver heart charms.

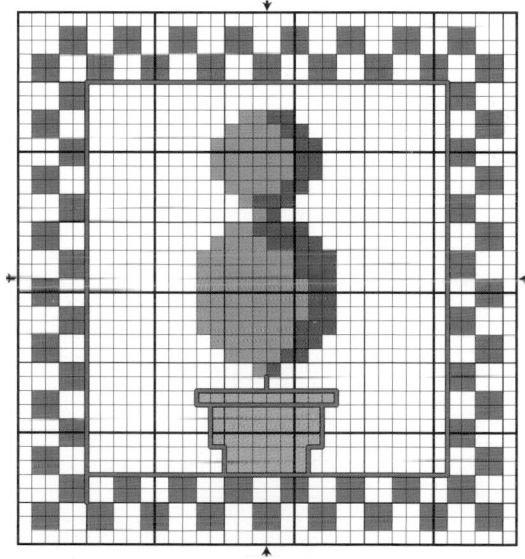

TOPIARY TREE CARD KEY

DMC stranded cotton

■ 413   ■ 500

■ 436   ■ 501

Backstitch ———— 413

NOTES

Stitch over two threads of cream 28 count linen with DMC stranded cottons, using two strands for cross stitch and one for backstitch.

SUNDIAL PICTURE

Sundials are often to be found in formal gardens as a focal point to draw the eye in. They are often very beautiful and in the past were important for telling the time.

DESIGN SIZE: 2¾ x 3in (7 x 7.5cm)
STITCH COUNT: 40 x 42

MATERIALS

- ❀ 6 x 7in (15 x 18cm) 28 count linen in lavender
- ❀ DMC stranded cottons as listed in the key
- ❀ Mill Hill white seed beads (Willow Fabrics)
- ❀ Beading needle
- ❀ Two small gold flower charms (Creative Beginnings)

1 Find the centre of the fabric and begin stitching here over two fabric threads following the chart on page 65. Use two strands of stranded cotton for the cross stitch and one for the backstitch.

2 When all the stitching is complete, sew on the charms and then the beads with the beading needle and matching thread. Press your embroidery carefully and frame.

sundial

FOUNTAIN PICTURE

Fountains are another important feature of the formal garden. They add a delightful and refreshing quality to a scene and can range from small and simple, as represented in this little design, to amazingly grand and elaborate.

DESIGN SIZE: 2¾ x 3in (7 x 7.5cm)
STITCH COUNT: 40 x 42

MATERIALS

- ❀ 6 x 7in (15 x 18cm) 28 count linen in lavender
- ❀ DMC stranded cottons as listed in the key
- ❀ Mill Hill white seed beads (Willow Fabrics)
- ❀ Beading needle
- ❀ Two small gold flower charms (Debbie Cripps)

1 Find the centre of the fabric and begin here over two fabric threads following the chart on page 65, using two strands of stranded cotton for the cross stitch and one for the backstitch.

2 When all the stitching is complete, sew on the charms and then the beads with the beading needle and matching thread. Press your embroidery carefully and frame.

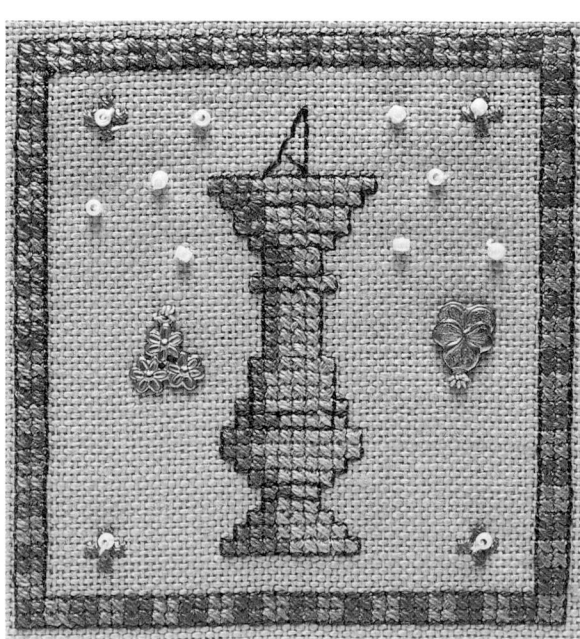

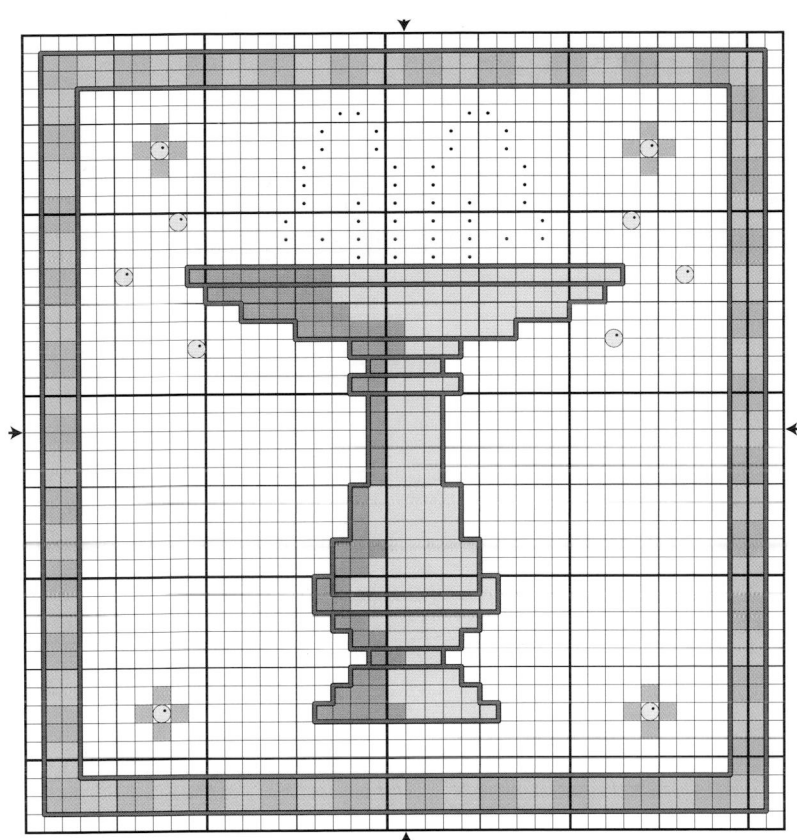

FOUNTAIN PICTURE KEY

DMC stranded cotton

■	340	■	927
■	554	·	BLANC
■	926		

Backstitch

———— 413

Beads

⊙ MILL HILL WHITE SEED BEADS

NOTES

Stitch over two threads of lavender 28 count linen with DMC stranded cottons, using two strands for cross stitch and one for backstitch.
Embellishments: two gold flower charms, white seed beads.

SUNDIAL PICTURE KEY

DMC stranded cotton

■	340	■	926
■	554	■	927

Backstitch

———— 413

Beads

⊙ MILL HILL WHITE SEED BEADS

NOTES

Stitch over two threads of lavender 28 count linen with DMC stranded cottons, using two strands for cross stitch and one for backstitch.
Embellishments: two gold flower charms, white seed beads.

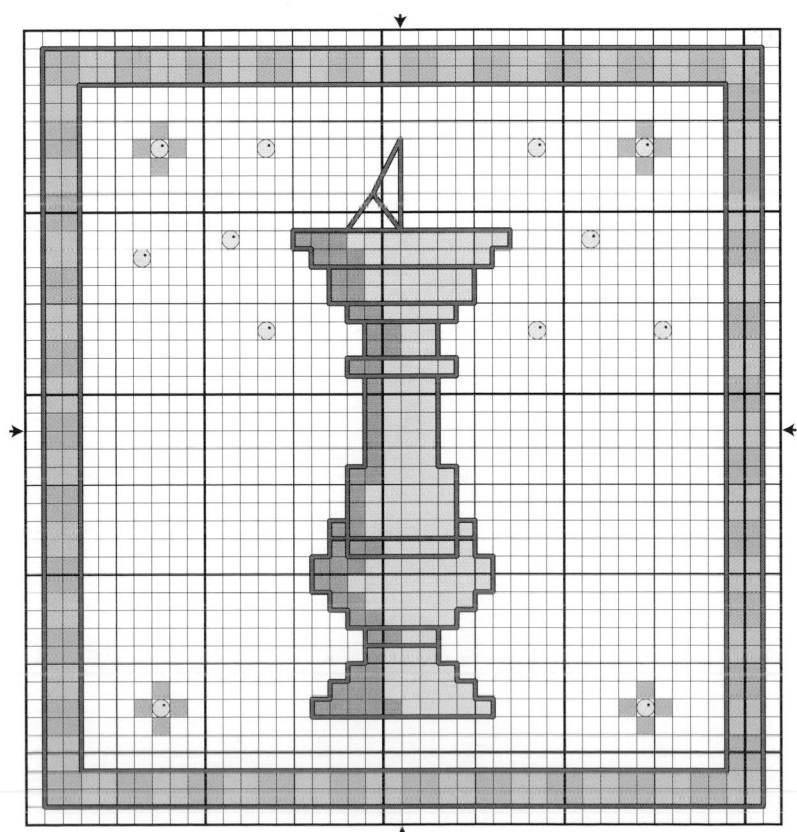

A GARDEN OF HERBS

 *Herb gardens are lovely places to wander, to enjoy their varied scents and textured foliage and the pots and containers in which herbs are often grown. There are so many herbs to choose from when considering a garden of herbs — herbs for culinary use, herbs with medicinal properties, herbs for use about the house. Most herbs are attractive plants in their own right. Many have interesting foliage, such as the variegated leaves of some sages or the feathery fronds of fennel. Many herbs have pretty flowers too, like the massed yellow and white daisy-like flowers of feverfew or the globular mauve heads of chives. Some of the more frequently grown herbs are featured in this chapter, made up into samplers, pictures, sachets and bags, and include lavender, rosemary, marjoram, chives, dill, thyme, camomile, basil, fennel, lovage and feverfew.*

HERB GARDEN SAMPLER

I have tried to show all the various elements of a herb garden in this sampler and have included plenty of busy, buzzing bees as they also have an important part to play in pollination.

DESIGN SIZE: 6 x 6in (15.2 x 15.2cm)
STITCH COUNT: 85 x 85

MATERIALS
- 12 x 12in (30 x 30cm) 28 count linen in sand
- DMC stranded cottons as listed in the key
- Gold butterfly charm (Debbie Cripps)
- Two gold bee charms (Heritage Stitchcraft)

1 Find the centre of the fabric and begin stitching here over two threads following the chart on page 68. Use two strands of stranded cotton for the cross stitch and one for backstitching and outlining. Use 469 to backstitch the herb stems and 501 for the herb names.

Outline the bees, rose flower, fence and flowerpots with 434. Use two strands for all French knots.

2 When all the stitching is complete, sew on the charms, then press your work carefully and frame.

HERB TALES
Herbs are supposed to be influenced by the moon and are best planted in the first quarter.

Rosemary grows best when a woman is in charge.

Basil will not grow well unless the gardener curses the plant as soon as it germinates.

Rosemary protects against lightning and injury.

Plant basil for a merry and cheerful heart.

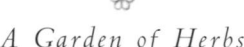

HERB GARDEN SAMPLER KEY

DMC stranded cotton

■ 310	■ 844
■ 434	■ 3348
■ 436	■ 3608
■ 469	■ 3820
■ 471	□ ECRU
▣ 501	■ 99 VARIEGATED

Backstitch

——	310
——	434
——	469
——	501
——	844

French knots

●	3348
●	3820
●	99 VARIEGATED

NOTES

Stitch over two threads of sand 28 count linen with DMC stranded cottons, using two strands for cross stitch and French knots and one strand for backstitching and outlining. Embellishments: gold butterfly charm and two gold bee charms.

DMC stranded cotton

■	208	■	413
■	209	■	420
+	210	■	437
□	211	□	ECRU
■	327	■	CARON WATERLILIES 'SPRUCE' 107
■	333		
■	340	■	CARON WATERLILIES 'AMETHYST' 006

Backstitch

——— 210 (LONG STITCH, HERB TIES AND SATIN STITCH BLOCKS)

——— 420

——— CARON WATERLILIES 'AMETHYST' 006

——— CARON WATERLILIES 'SPRUCE' 107

Beads

● MILL HILL PURPLE SEED BEADS

NOTES

Stitch over two threads of white 28 count linen with DMC stranded cottons, using two strands for cross stitch and one for backstitch. Use one strand of Caron thread throughout. Use long stitch for the ties on the bunches of herbs and satin stitch for the row below. Embellishments: purple seed beads.

LAVENDER SAMPLER

Lavender is one of my favourite plants as I love both the colour and the fragrance. It has been used for centuries, made into lavender bags and hung in wardrobes, placed between the sheets in linen cupboards, made into oils, soaps and eau de cologne and of course pot pourri. Today, lavender is as popular as ever and the new interest in aromatherapy and the special properties of different plant oils mean that the soothing properties of lavender are still highly regarded.

soothing lavender

DESIGN SIZE: 5⅛ x 9¼in (13 x 23.5cm)
STITCH COUNT: 72 x 131

MATERIALS

- 10 x 18in (25.5 x 46cm) 28 count linen in white
- DMC stranded cottons as listed in the key
- Caron Waterlilies threads 'Amethyst' 006 and 'Spruce' 107
- Size 26 tapestry needle
- Mill Hill purple seed beads (No.00252)
- Beading needle

1 Find the centre of the fabric and begin stitching here over two threads following the chart on page 69. Use two strands of stranded cotton for the cross stitch and one for the backstitching and outlining. Use one strand for the Caron threads throughout.

2 When all the stitching is complete sew on the seed beads using the beading needle, then press your embroidery carefully and frame.

Many attractive cards could be made from the individual motifs in the delightful Lavender Sampler, sachet and bags. You could also stitch the motifs from the lavender bags, repeating them along a towel or tea towel border

LAVENDER SACHET

This pretty sachet (shown on page 70) would be perfect to give as a gift to someone special or to place amongst your clothes for delicate fragrance.

DESIGN SIZE: 2¼ x 2⅞in (5.7 x 7.2cm)
STITCH COUNT: 32 x 40

MATERIALS

❀ Two pieces of 8 x 6in (20 x 15cm) 28 count linen in white
❀ DMC stranded cottons as listed in the key
❀ Size 26 tapestry needle
❀ White lace 1¼in (3cm) wide x 6in (15cm)
❀ White sewing cotton
❀ Mill Hill purple seed beads (No.00252)
❀ Beading needle
❀ Polyester filling
❀ Dried lavender in small muslin bag
❀ Lilac gingham ribbon 12in (30cm)

1 Take one of the pieces of linen, find the centre and begin stitching here over two fabric threads using only one strand of stranded cotton. Follow the chart on page 73, using the left-hand design.

2 When all the stitching is complete, sew on the length of lace below the last row of stitching using white sewing cotton. Then sew on the seed beads using the beading needle.

DRYING LAVENDER

Pick the lavender flowers when fresh and the weather is dry. Cut the stems and tie with string then hang the bunches in a cool, airy place. When dried, lavender can be used for flower arrangements or added to lavender bags. Dried lavender is fragile so it is best to place it out of reach.

aromatic lavender

3 Make up the sachet by stitching a small hem at the top of the front and back pieces. Measure 1in (2.5cm) down and withdraw three threads to make the ribbon row. Sew up the sides and bottom of the bag, trim the seams and clip the corners.

4 Press carefully then turn the bag right way out and thread the ribbon through. Fill with stuffing, add the dried lavender then pull up the ribbon and tie in a bow.

LAVENDER BAGS

These tiny lavender bags (shown on page 71) have an old-fashioned appeal and remind me of the antique linen that can be found in French markets.

Small Lavender Bag

DESIGN SIZE: 1¹⁄₁₆ x 1³⁄₁₆in (2.7 x 2.2cm)
STITCH COUNT: 15 x 12

MATERIALS

❀ Two 3¾ x 3¼in (9.5 x 8cm) pieces of 28 count linen in natural
❀ DMC stranded cottons as listed in the key
❀ Size 26 tapestry needle
❀ Sewing cotton to match linen
❀ Narrow lilac ribbon 8in (20cm)
❀ Polyester filling and dried lavender

1 Take one of the pieces of linen and stitch the design in the centre over two fabric threads using the chart on page 73. Use two strands of stranded cotton for the cross stitch and one for the backstitch.

2 Make up the bag by using matching sewing cotton to make a small hem at the top of each piece of linen. Withdraw three threads ½in (1.25cm) down on each piece for the ribbon row. Placing right sides together, sew up the sides and bottom of the bag, trim the seams and clip the corners.

3 Press the bag, turn right way out and stuff firmly with polyester filling, adding the dried lavender. Thread the ribbon through and tie in a bow.

Large Lavender Bag

DESIGN SIZE: 3/16 x 13/16in (3 x 2.2cm)
STITCH COUNT: 12 x 17

MATERIALS

- Two 5 x 3¼in (12.5 x 8cm) pieces of 28 count linen in natural
- DMC stranded cottons as listed in the key
- Size 26 tapestry needle
- Sewing cotton to match linen
- Narrow lilac ribbon 8in (20cm)
- Polyester filling
- Dried lavender

1 Take one of the pieces of linen and stitch the design in the centre over two fabric threads using the chart below. Use two strands of stranded cotton for the cross stitch and one for the backstitch.

2 Make up the bag by using matching sewing cotton to make a small hem at the top of each piece of linen. Withdraw three threads ½in (1.25cm) down on each piece for the ribbon row. Placing right sides together, sew up the sides and bottom of the bag, trim the seams and clip the corners.

3 Press the bag, turn right way out and stuff firmly with polyester filling, adding the dried lavender. Thread the ribbon through and tie in a bow.

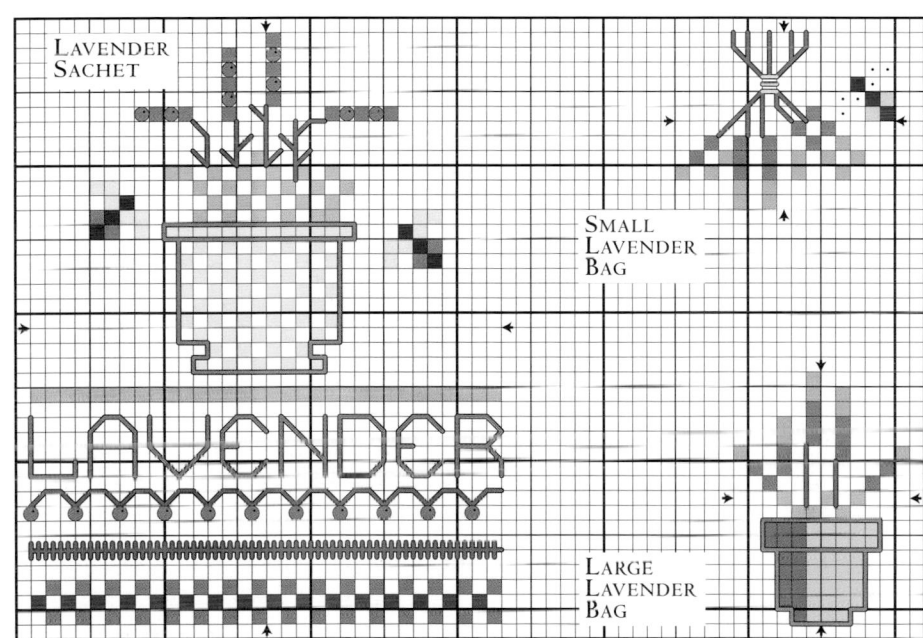

LAVENDER SACHET AND BAGS KEY

DMC stranded cotton

333	437	842
340	501	· BLANC
413	502	
420	612	

Beads

Ⓜ MILL HILL PURPLE SEED BEADS

Backstitch

——	210
——	333
——	502
——	612

NOTES

Stitch the Sachet over two threads of white 28 count linen with one strand of DMC stranded cotton. Embellishments: purple seed beads and white lace.

Stitch the two Bags over two threads of natural 28 count linen, using two strands for cross stitch, one for backstitch.

FOUR HERB PICTURES

I have chosen four popular herbs to form a set of small pictures that could be hung together in the kitchen or dining room.

Thyme Picture

DESIGN SIZE: 1¾ x 2¼in (4.5 x 5.7cm)
STITCH COUNT: 25 x 32

MATERIALS

- 6 x 5in (15 x 12.5cm) 28 count linen in raw linen
- DMC stranded cottons as listed in the key
- Size 26 tapestry needle
- Gold bee charm (Heritage Stitchcraft)

1 Find the centre of the fabric and begin stitching here over two fabric threads following the chart on page 76, using two strands of stranded cotton for the cross stitch and one for the backstitching and outlining.

2 When all the stitching is complete, sew on the bee charm with matching sewing cotton. Now press your embroidery and frame it.

Marjoram Picture

DESIGN SIZE: 2⅛ x 2¾in (5.5 x 7.2cm)
STITCH COUNT: 30 x 40

MATERIALS

- 6 x 5in (15 x 12.5cm) 28 count linen in raw linen
- DMC stranded cottons as listed in the key
- Size 26 tapestry needle
- Gold bee charm (Heritage Stitchcraft)

1 Find the centre of the fabric and begin stitching here over two fabric threads, following the chart on page 76. Use two strands of stranded cotton for the cross stitch, French knots and backstitch stems and one strand for the backstitch outlining and lettering.

2 When all the stitching is completed, sew on the bee charm with matching sewing cotton, then press your embroidery and frame it.

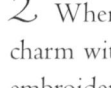

MARJORAM
Pot marjoram, sweet marjoram and wild marjoram are useful herbs for cooking and are good with meat, seafood and vegetables. When dried they are often used in pasta dishes and pizzas.

useful herbs

chives Picture

DESIGN SIZE: 1⅞ x 2⅝in (4.8 x 6.8cm)
STITCH COUNT: 26 x 38

MATERIALS

- ❀ 6 x 5in (15 x 12.5cm) 28 count linen in raw linen
- ❀ DMC stranded cottons as listed in the key
- ❀ Size 26 tapestry needle
- ❀ Gold butterfly charm (Debbie Cripps)

1 Find the centre of the fabric and begin stitching here over two linen threads following the chart given on page 77. Use two strands of stranded cotton for all the cross stitch and one strand for the backstitching and outlining.

2 When all the stitching is complete, sew on the butterfly charm with matching sewing cotton, then press your embroidery and frame it.

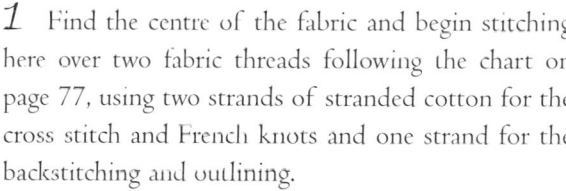

CHIVES
Chives are used for their mild onion flavour and are often just chopped straight onto new potatoes or into salads. Their leaves can be used to flavour many dishes.

Dill Picture

DESIGN SIZE: 1⁵⁄₁₆ x 2⅜in (3.4 x 6.1cm)
STITCH COUNT: 18 x 33

MATERIALS

- ❀ 6 x 5in (15 x 12.5cm) 28 count linen in raw linen
- ❀ DMC stranded cottons as listed in the key
- ❀ Size 26 tapestry needle
- ❀ Two gold butterfly charms (Debbie Cripps)

1 Find the centre of the fabric and begin stitching here over two fabric threads following the chart on page 77, using two strands of stranded cotton for the cross stitch and French knots and one strand for the backstitching and outlining.

2 When all the stitching is complete, sew on the butterfly charms with matching sewing cotton, then press your embroidery and frame it.

DILL
Dill is delicious in sauces with fish and also chopped into salads. The seeds are used in pickling, especially with pickled cucumbers and in chutneys.

freshly picked

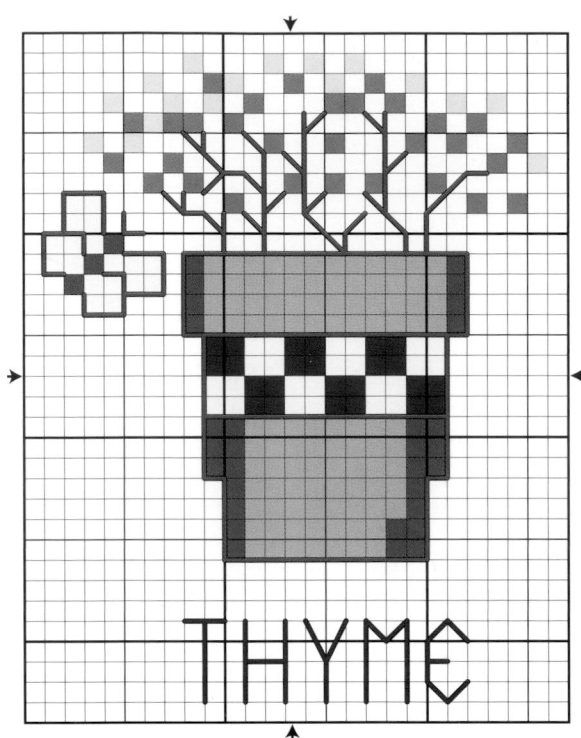

MARJORAM PICTURE KEY

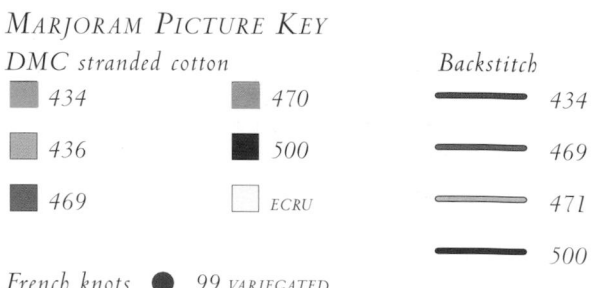

DMC stranded cotton

				Backstitch
■ 434		■ 470		—— 434
■ 436		■ 500		—— 469
■ 469		□ ECRU		—— 471
				—— 500

French knots ● 99 VARIEGATED

NOTES

Stitch over two threads of raw 28 count linen with DMC
stranded cottons, using two strands for cross stitch and French
knots and one strand for backstitch.
Embellishments: gold bee charm.

THYME PICTURE KEY

DMC stranded cotton

			Backstitch
■ 434	■ 3607		—— 434
■ 436	□ 3609		—— 500
■ 500	□ ECRU		
■ 501			

NOTES

Stitch over two threads of raw 28 count linen with DMC
stranded cottons, using two strands for cross stitch and one for
backstitch.
Embellishments: gold bee charm.

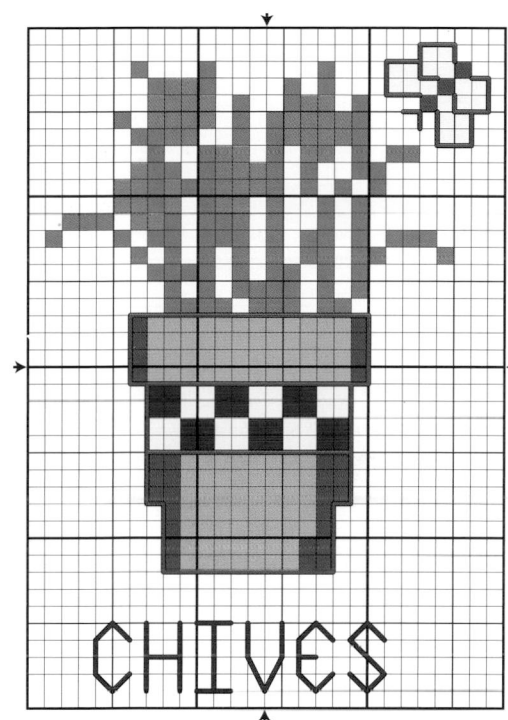

DILL PICTURE KEY

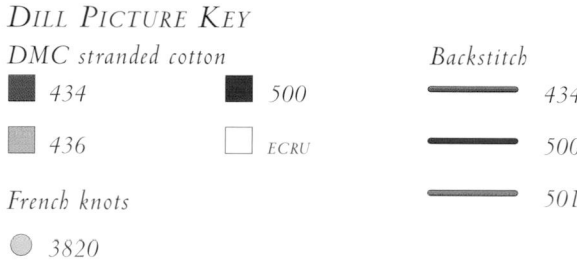

DMC stranded cotton		Backstitch	
■ 434	■ 500	— 434	
■ 436	□ ECRU	— 500	

French knots

● 3820

─ 501

NOTES

Stitch over two threads of raw 28 count linen with DMC stranded cottons, using two strands for cross stitch and French knots and one strand for backstitch.
Embellishments: two gold butterfly charms.

CHIVES PICTURE KEY

DMC stranded cotton		Backstitch	
■ 434	■ 501	— 434	
■ 436	■ 553	— 500	
■ 500	□ ECRU		

NOTES

Stitch over two threads of raw 28 count linen with DMC stranded cottons, using two strands for cross stitch and one for backstitch.
Embellishments: gold butterfly charm.

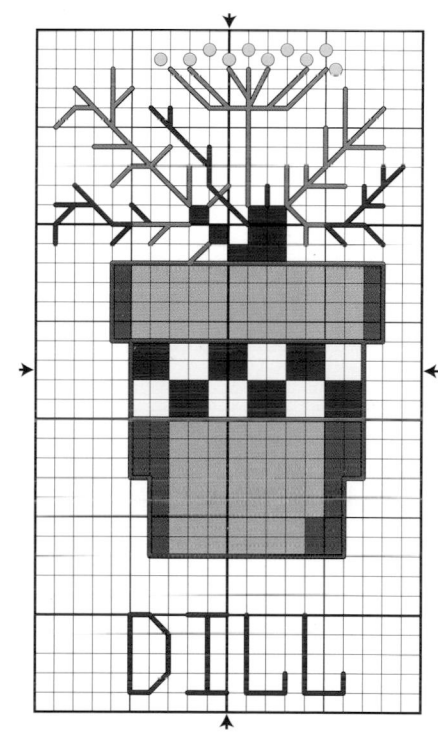

HERB PILLOW

This lace-edged pillow could be placed on top of bed pillows, to look pretty and to scent the air with soothing herbs to promote relaxation and peaceful sleep.

DESIGN SIZE: 3¾ x 8¾in (9.5 x 22.2cm)

STITCH COUNT: 127 x 54

MATERIALS

❀ 12 x 7in (30 x 18cm) 28 count linen in white
❀ DMC stranded cottons as listed in the key
❀ Size 26 tapestry needle
❀ Two Mill Hill pansy buttons (American Country Cross Stitch)
❀ Two pieces of fine white cotton fabric 3¾ x 9in (9.5 x 23cm)
❀ Polyester filling
❀ Dried sweet-scented herbs of your choice
❀ Ruched white lace ¾in (2cm) wide x 28in (70cm)
❀ Black and white sewing cotton

fragrant bouquet

HERBAL POT POURRI

Dry rose leaves, petals, clove carnations, lavender, woodruff, rosemary and orange blossom between sheets of tissue paper in a warm, dark place. Take ¼oz (5g) of cloves, 2oz (50g) of powdered orris root, the finely pared rind of one lemon and one orange, two bay leaves, a sprig of myrtle, rosemary and lemon thyme and a handful of lavender flowers. Place in a large bowl and add two drops of each of the following essential oils: musk, lavender, lemon and jasmine. Mix all the ingredients together, then place in a lidded jar. After storing for six weeks, make up into sachets to keep among clothes, or place in a herb pillow.

1 Find the centre of the fabric and stitch over two fabric threads following the chart on page 80, using two strands of stranded cotton for the cross stitch.

2 When all the stitching is complete sew on the pansy buttons, if you are using them, using black sewing cotton to form the markings in the centre. If you are not using the buttons, then stitch the motifs from the chart instead. When the stitching is complete, press your work carefully.

3 To make up the cushion pad, take the two pieces of white cotton fabric, place them right sides together

and sew round three sides with white sewing cotton. Turn right way out and stuff firmly with polyester filling and herbs of your choice – dried lavender, rose petals and thyme are all lovely. Sew up the fourth side.

4 To make up the pillow, take the second piece of white linen, place it right sides together with the embroidered piece and sew around three sides. Clip the corners and trim the edges, then press carefully. Turn the right way out, insert the cushion pad and then sew up the fourth side. Using the white sewing cotton, sew on the lace all round the edges to complete.

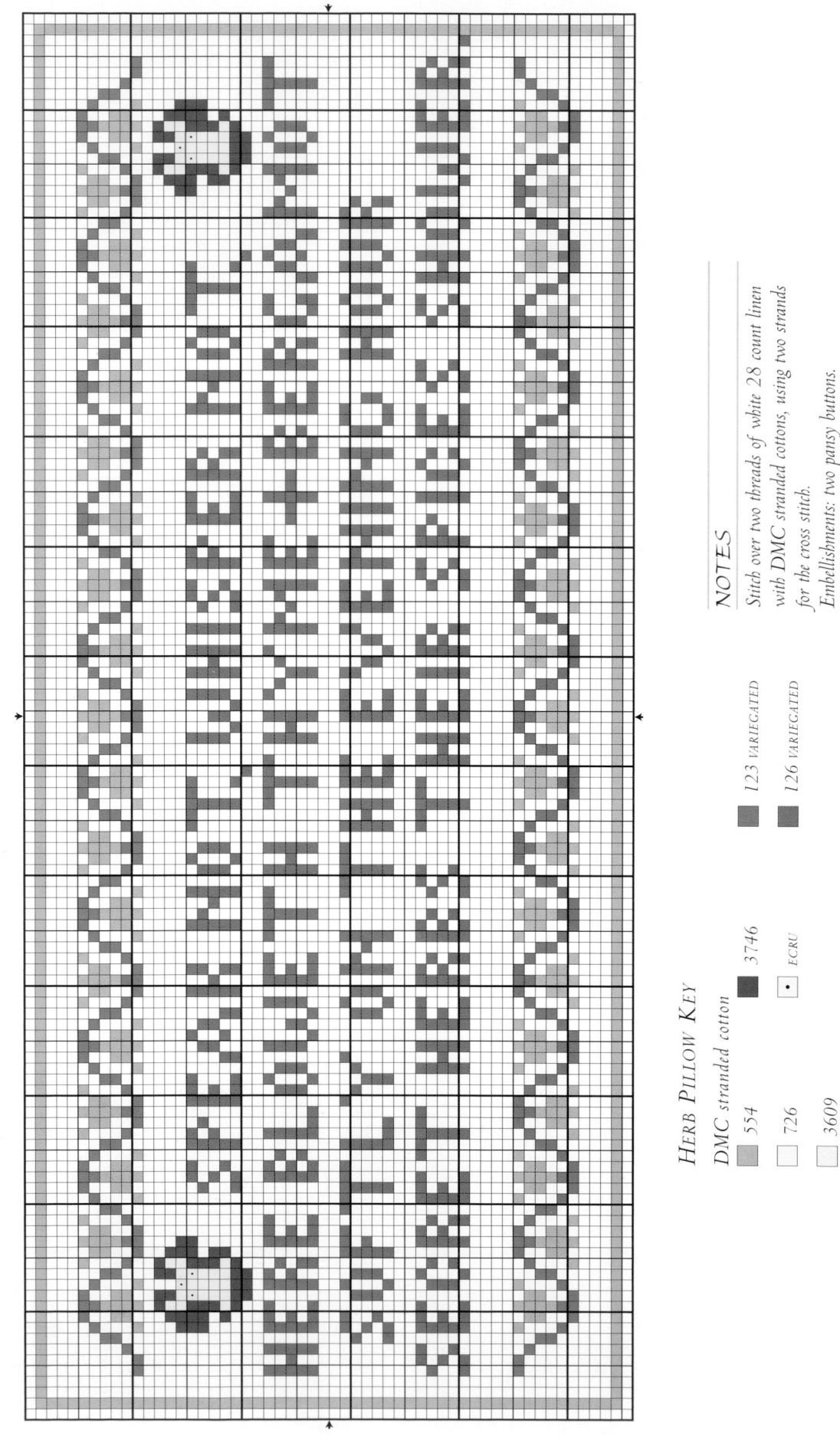

HERB PILLOW KEY

DMC stranded cotton

■ 554	■ 3746	■ 123 *VARIEGATED*
□ 726	• ECRU	■ 126 *VARIEGATED*
□ 3609		

NOTES

Stitch over two threads of white 28 count linen with DMC stranded cottons, using two strands for the cross stitch.
Embellishments: two pansy buttons.

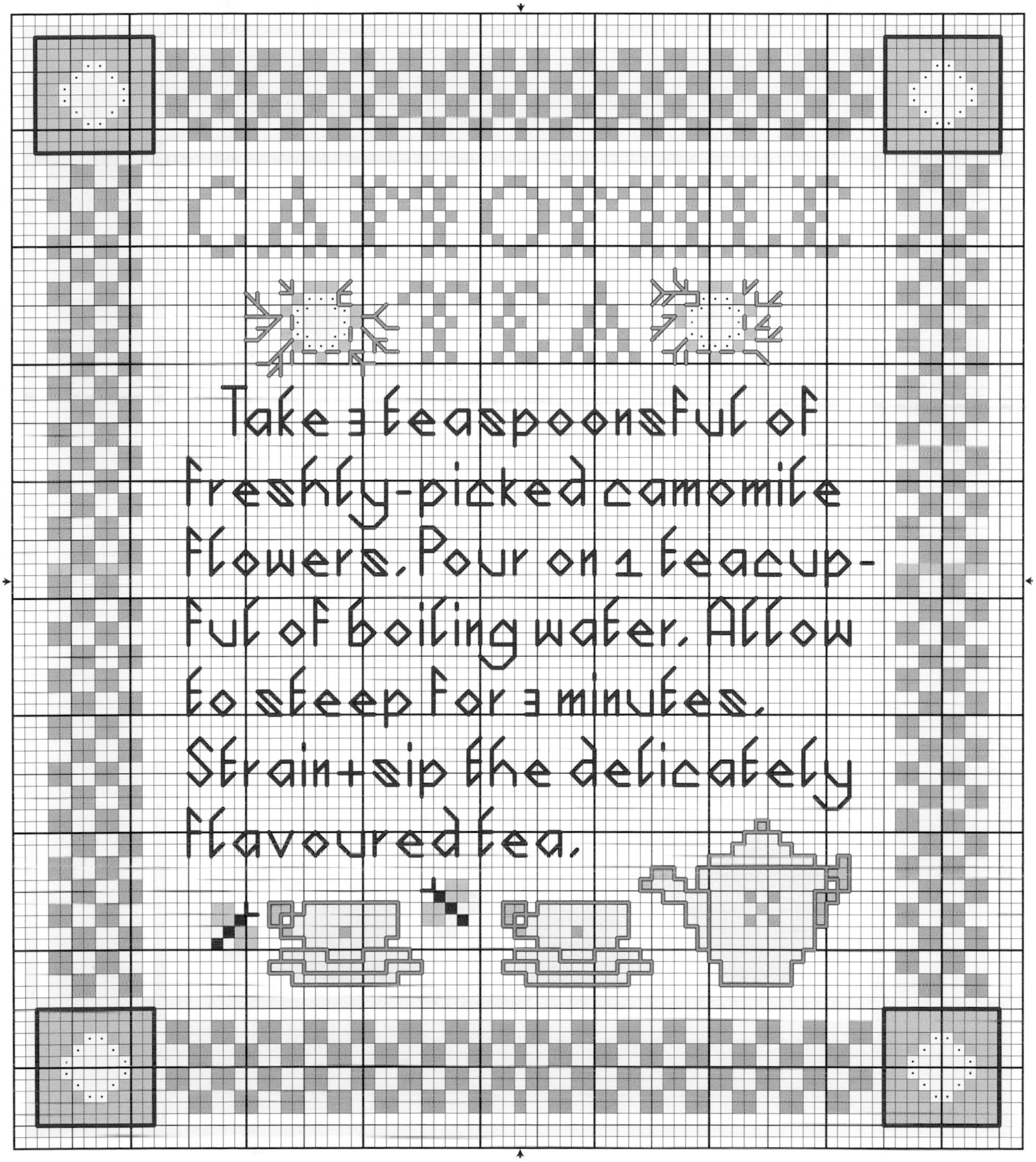

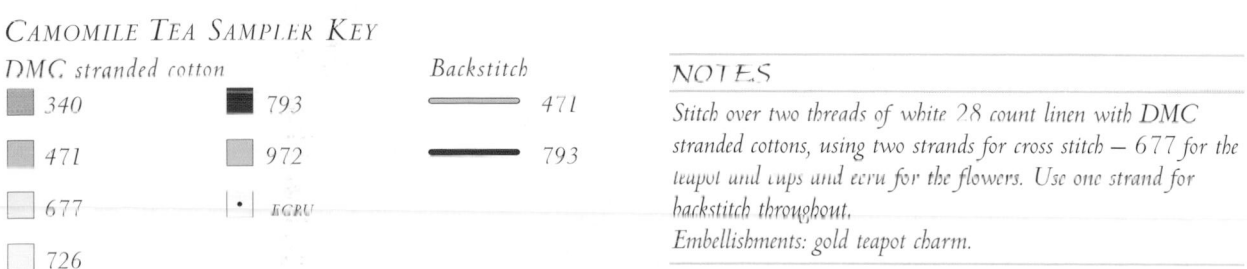

Take 3 teaspoonsful of freshly-picked camomile flowers. Pour on 1 teacupful of boiling water. Allow to steep for 3 minutes. Strain+sip the delicately flavoured tea.

CAMOMILE TEA SAMPLER KEY

DMC stranded cotton

▨ 340	▨ 793
▨ 471	▨ 972
▨ 677	· ECRU
▨ 726	

Backstitch

— 471

— 793

NOTES

Stitch over two threads of white 28 count linen with DMC stranded cottons, using two strands for cross stitch — 677 for the teapot and cups and ecru for the flowers. Use one strand for backstitch throughout.

Embellishments: gold teapot charm.

CAMOMILE TEA SAMPLER

Many herbs are used to make tea and camomile is one of the most popular. Camomile tea is soothing and sleep-inducing and is therefore especially good when taken at night. Camomile can be grown in a pot or in the flower border. There is another form of camomile which is often planted to make a lawn as it is robust and sweet-scented, but it does not produce flowers.

DESIGN SIZE: 6 x 6¾in (15.2 x 17.2cm)
STITCH COUNT: 85 x 95

MATERIALS

* 9 x 11in (23 x 28cm) 28 count linen in white
* DMC stranded cottons as listed in the key
* Size 26 tapestry needle
* Gold teapot charm (Debbie Cripps)

1 Find the centre of the fabric and begin stitching here over two fabric threads following the chart on page 81, using two strands of stranded cotton for the cross stitch and one strand for the backstitch.

2 When all the stitching is complete, sew on the charm using matching thread, then press your embroidery carefully and frame it.

relaxing camomile

HERBAL TEA

Today, herbal teas are enjoyed as a healthy and refreshing drink, though in the past they were a form of medicine and all kinds of healing properties were claimed for them. Some of the favourite herbal teas are rosehip, feverfew, peppermint, lemon thyme, fennel and perhaps most of all, camomile.

CAMOMILE
★ TEA ★

Take a teaspoonful of
freshly picked camomile
flowers. Pour on a teacupful of boiling water. Allow
to steep for a minute.
Strain + sip the delicately
flavoured tea.

BIRDS AND BEES

garden visitors

Much of the joy of gardening comes from watching the many garden visitors, particularly birds, bees and butterflies, and these creatures, and more, are captured in the designs in this chapter, which include samplers, pictures, cards, a fridge magnet, a towel border and a box.

People have had close affinities with birds since ancient times and folklore beliefs still influence attitudes today. It was believed that birds had magical qualities and by observing them people thought it was possible to foretell the future, the weather and even disasters. Birds were linked to fertility, perhaps because of their obvious courtship and nest-building activities. They were also important in witchcraft and were used in strange cures for all kinds of ailments.

There is also a great deal of folklore surrounding bees and today their contribution to the garden is well known and valued. Certain plants like buddleia encourage this useful little insect.

BIRD SAMPLER

I decided to design a band sampler about birds in a pretty and decorative contemporary style. The idea of singing birds and bird-song developed as the sampler progressed. The sound of bird-song is one of the joys of gardening as is the sight of birds perching, flying and nesting.

DESIGN SIZE: 5¹⁄₁₆ x 10¾in (13 x 27.5cm)
STITCH COUNT: 71 x 151

MATERIALS

- 10 x 20in (25.5 x 51cm) 28 count linen in pale pink
- DMC stranded cottons as listed in the key
- Size 26 tapestry needle
- Mill Hill white dove button (American Country Cross Stitch)
- Two Mill Hill red bird buttons

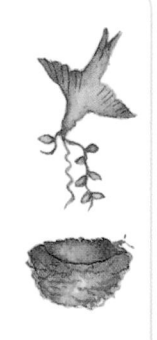

BIRD PROVERBS

Birds are often referred to in proverbs which date back centuries. Some of the many still in use include, 'A bird in the hand is worth two in the bush', 'Birds of a feather flock together', 'The early bird catches the worm' and 'Fine feathers make fine birds'.

1 Find the centre of the fabric and begin stitching here over two threads following the chart on pages 86/87. Use two strands of stranded cotton for the cross stitch and one for the backstitching and outlining.

2 When the stitching is complete sew on the buttons with matching thread if you are using them. If not, stitch the motifs from the chart instead. Once finished, press your embroidery carefully and frame it.

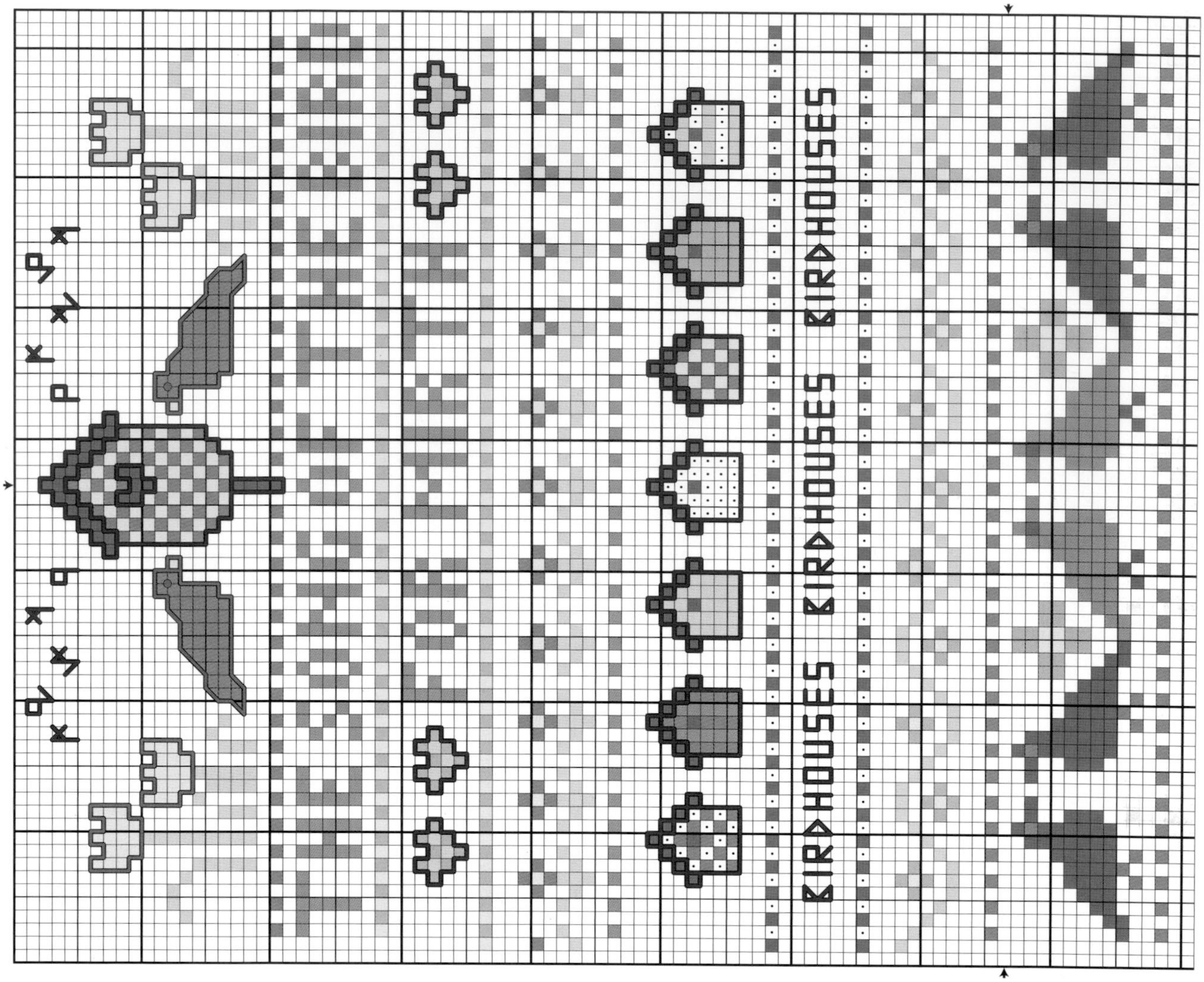

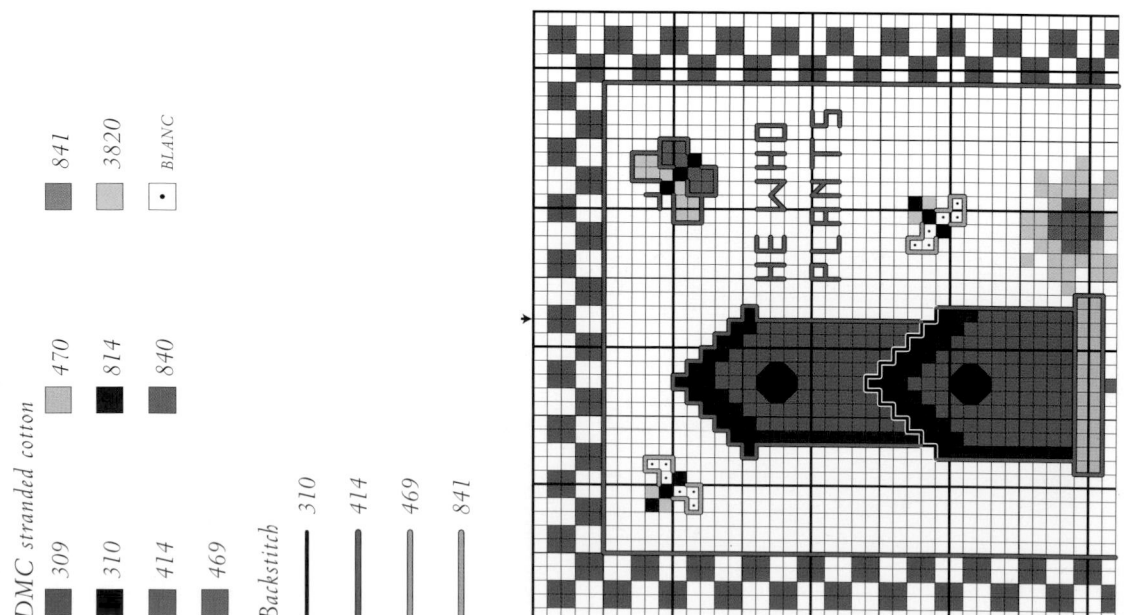

Tall Birdhouse Sampler Key

DMC *stranded cotton*

309	470	841
310	814	3820
414	840	• BLANC
469		

Backstitch

— 310
— 414
— 469
— 841

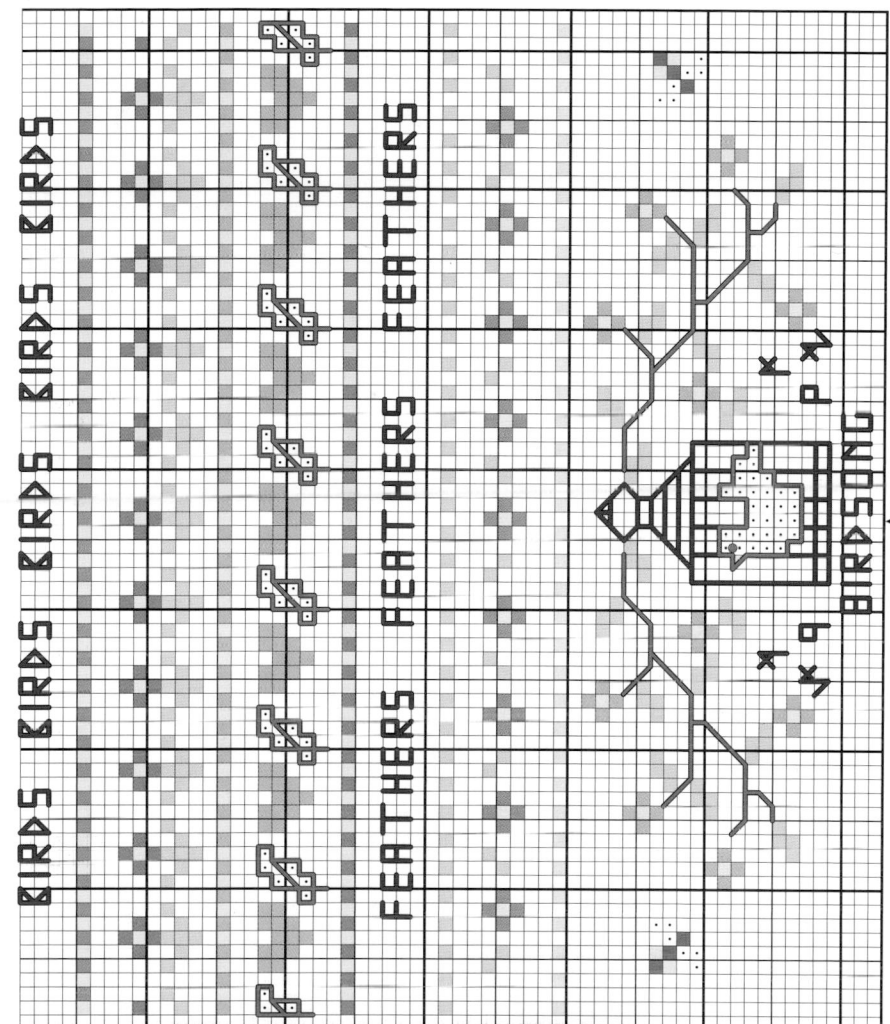

BIRD SAMPLER KEY

DMC stranded cotton

■ 351		■ 597	
□ 368		■ 646	
▨ 554		▨ 3047	

Backstitch

— 413

— 646

· BLANC

French knots

● 646

NOTES

Stitch over two threads of pale pink 28 count linen with DMC stranded cottons, using two strands for cross stitch and one for backstitch. Embellishments: white dove button, two red bird buttons.

NOTES

Stitch over two threads of cream 28 count linen with DMC stranded cottons, using two strands for cross stitch. Use two strands of 469 for the backstitch flower stems and one strand for remaining backstitch colours. Embellishments: silver fork charm and silver trowel charm.

FOUR SEASONAL BIRDHOUSES

Birdhouses are very popular and evocative images and so decorative that I decided to stitch a set of small seasonal birdhouses in a folk-art style, with added charms for extra interest. The distinctive shape of the birdhouse can be seen at all times of year in the garden and lends itself particularly well to cross stitch interpretation.

spring birdhouse

spring Birdhouse Picture

DESIGN SIZE: 2¾ x 3in (7 x 7.5cm)
STITCH COUNT: 39 x 41

MATERIALS

- ❀ 6 x 6in (15 x 15cm) 28 count linen in white
- ❀ DMC stranded cottons as listed in the key
- ❀ Size 26 tapestry needle
- ❀ Two gold dragonfly charms (Heritage Stitchcraft)

1 Find the centre of the fabric and begin stitching over two fabric threads following the chart on page 90, using two strands of stranded cotton for the cross stitch and one strand for the backstitching and outlining.

2 When the stitching is complete sew on the charms with matching sewing cotton, then press your embroidery and frame it.

bluebird

Summer Birdhouse Picture

DESIGN SIZE: 2¾ x 3in (7 x 7.5cm)
STITCH COUNT: 39 x 41

MATERIALS

- ❀ 6 x 6in (15 x 15cm) 28 count linen in cream
- ❀ DMC stranded cottons as listed in the key
- ❀ Size 26 tapestry needle
- ❀ Two gold bee charms (Heritage Stitchcraft)

1 Find the centre of the fabric and begin stitching over two fabric threads following the chart on page 90, using two strands of stranded cotton for the cross stitch and one strand for the backstitching and outlining.

2 When the stitching is complete sew on the charms with matching sewing cotton, then press your embroidery and frame it.

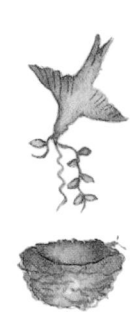

1 Find the centre of the fabric and begin stitching over two fabric threads following the chart on page 91, using two strands of stranded cotton for the cross stitch and one strand for the backstitching and outlining.

2 When the stitching is complete sew on the charms with matching sewing cotton, then press your embroidery and frame it.

Autumn Birdhouse Picture

DESIGN SIZE: 2¾ x 3in (7 x 7.5cm)

STITCH COUNT: 39 x 41

MATERIALS

❀ 6 x 6in (15 x 15cm) 28 count linen in sand
❀ DMC stranded cottons as listed in the key
❀ Size 26 tapestry needle
❀ Two gold leaf charms (Creative Beginnings)

Winter Birdhouse Picture

DESIGN SIZE: 2¾ x 3in (7 x 7.5cm)

STITCH COUNT: 39 x 41

MATERIALS

❀ 6 x 6in (15 x 15cm) 28 count linen in misty blue
❀ DMC stranded cottons as listed in the key
❀ Size 26 tapestry needle
❀ Two gold snowflake charms (Creative Beginnings)

robin

1 Find the centre of the fabric and begin stitching over two fabric threads following the chart on page 91, using two strands of stranded cotton for the cross stitch and one strand for the backstitching and outlining.

2 When the stitching is complete sew on the charms with matching sewing cotton, then press your embroidery and frame it.

SPRING BIRDHOUSE PICTURE KEY

DMC stranded cotton

- 309
- 317
- 341
- 434
- 445
- 911
- 3609
- 3747

Backstitch

- ——— 309
- ——— 317
- ——— 434
- ——— 911

French knots

- ● 317

NOTES

Stitch over two threads of white 28 count linen with DMC stranded cottons, using two strands for cross stitch and one for backstitch. Embellishments: two gold dragonfly charms.

SUMMER BIRDHOUSE PICTURE KEY

DMC stranded cotton

- 209
- 211
- 413
- 434
- 725
- 958
- 3607

Backstitch

- ——— 413
- ——— 3607

NOTES

Stitch over two threads of cream 28 count linen with DMC stranded cottons, using two strands for cross stitch and one for backstitch. Embellishments: two gold bee charms.

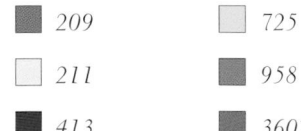

AUTUMN BIRDHOUSE PICTURE KEY

DMC stranded cotton

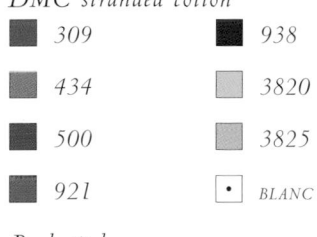

■	309	■	938
■	434	■	3820
■	500	■	3825
■	921	・	BLANC

Backstitch

―――――― 309   ―――――― 938

NOTES

Stitch over two threads of sand 28 count linen with DMC stranded cottons, using two strands for cross stitch and one for backstitch. Embellishments: two gold leaf charms.

WINTER BIRDHOUSE PICTURE KEY

DMC stranded cotton

■	309	■	930
■	413	■	3755
■	434	・	BLANC
■	500		

Backstitch

―――――― 413   ━━━━▷ BLANC

―――――― 930

NOTES

Stitch over two threads of blue 28 count linen with DMC stranded cottons, using two strands for cross stitch and one for backstitch. Use 413 to outline the birdhouse and 930 for the backstitch lettering. Embellishments: two gold snowflake charms.

TALL BIRDHOUSE SAMPLER

This birdhouse is one of the 'multi-storied' kind that frequently appear in folk-art designs. It is a fun piece with a contemporary feel.

DESIGN SIZE: 3 x 6in (7.5 x 15.2cm)
STITCH COUNT: 42 x 86

MATERIALS

❀ 6 x 10in (15 x 25.5cm) 28 count linen in cream
❀ DMC stranded cottons as listed in the key
❀ Size 26 tapestry needle
❀ Silver fork charm (Debbie Cripps)
❀ Silver trowel charm (Debbie Cripps)

1 Find the centre of the fabric and begin stitching here over two threads following the chart on pages 86/87. Use two strands of stranded cotton for the cross stitch and one for the backstitching and outlining. Use two strands for the backstitch flower stems.

2 When the stitching is complete, sew on the charms with matching sewing cotton if you are using them, then press your embroidery and frame it.

FEATHERING THEIR NESTS 
It is thought that people feel an affinity to birds because they build homes as humans do. Nests are very varied, but each species of bird builds to a set, instinctive plan. Their choice of location sometimes causes amusement as does their choice of materials. Although they use mud, twigs and other natural materials, birds also make good use of plastic twine, tissue, foil and paper. The cup-shaped nest built by many birds offers protection to the eggs.

BUTTERFLIES AND LADYBIRDS PICTURE

The creatures in this picture have a childlike appeal, and you could use single motifs from the design on other items. They could also be stitched onto children's clothing using waste canvas or be added to household linen.

ATTRACTING BUTTERFLIES

To attract butterflies to your garden, try growing buddleia – also known as the 'butterfly bush' – and in the summer this pretty shrub will be covered in insects feasting on its nectar.

DESIGN SIZE: 4 x 4⅝in (10 x 11.8cm)
STITCH COUNT: 57 x 66

MATERIALS

❀ 7 x 8in (18 x 20cm) 28 count linen in white
❀ DMC stranded cottons as listed in the key
❀ Size 26 tapestry needle

1 Find the centre of the fabric and begin stitching here over two fabric threads following the chart on page 101. Use two strands of stranded cotton for the cross stitch and one for the backstitch and the French knots.

2 When all the stitching is complete press your work carefully and frame.

BEEHIVE SAMPLER

I love bees and beehives so I wanted to produce a sampler celebrating both. I searched for a quotation to incorporate and was pleased to discover such an appropriate one in an old poetry book.

DESIGN SIZE: 4⅞ x 9¼in (12.3 x 23.4cm)
STITCH COUNT: 67 x 131

MATERIALS

honeybees

- ❀ 8 x 16in (20 x 40cm) 28 count linen in cream
- ❀ DMC stranded cottons as listed in the key
- ❀ Size 26 tapestry needle
- ❀ Gold bee charm (Heritage Stitchcraft)

1 Find the centre of the fabric and begin stitching here over two fabric threads following the chart on page 96. Use two strands of stranded cotton for the cross stitch and one for the backstitch.

2 When all the stitching is complete sew on the charm with matching thread (see picture opposite), then press your embroidery carefully and frame it.

YELLOW BEEHIVE CARD

This design (shown on page 97) has a bright and contemporary appearance with its cheery blue and white check border. It could also be framed as a picture.

DESIGN SIZE: 3 x 2½in (7.5 x 6.3cm)
STITCH COUNT: 40 x 36

MATERIALS

- ❀ 6 x 6in (15 x 15cm) 28 count linen in white
- ❀ DMC stranded cottons as listed in the key
- ❀ Size 26 tapestry needle
- ❀ White card with aperture 3 x 3in (7.5 x 7.5cm)

1 Find the centre of the fabric and begin stitching here over two fabric threads following the chart on page 97. Use two strands of stranded cotton for the cross stitch and one for the backstitching and outlining.

2 When complete, press the embroidery carefully and make up the card (see page 125).

BEEHIVES CARD

This design (shown on page 97) has an old-fashioned feel, featuring rows of beehives or skeps on shelves which was how they used to be kept in gardens of the past.

DESIGN SIZE: 1⅞ x 2¾in (4.8 x 7cm)
STITCH COUNT: 31 x 50

MATERIALS

- ❀ 3 x 5in (8 x 12.5cm) 28 count linen in sand
- ❀ DMC stranded cottons as listed in the key
- ❀ Size 26 tapestry needle
- ❀ Cream card with aperture 2¼ x 3in (5.5 x 7.5cm)

1 Find the centre of the fabric and begin stitching here over two fabric threads following the chart on page 97. Use two strands of stranded cotton for the cross stitch and one for the backstitching and outlining.

2 When all the stitching is complete, press carefully and make up into the card (see page 125).

BEE LORE

In past times most gardens had a beehive tucked away somewhere. Bees were kept for honey and beeswax, which was valued for candles and polish, and bees were regarded with affection and treated with respect. Some people still believe you should go and tell the bees any important news, such as a birth or death in the family.

ABCDEFGHI
KLMNOPQR
STUVWXYZ

The bee is small among
winged
creatures

Yet her produce takes
first place
for
sweetness

1234567890

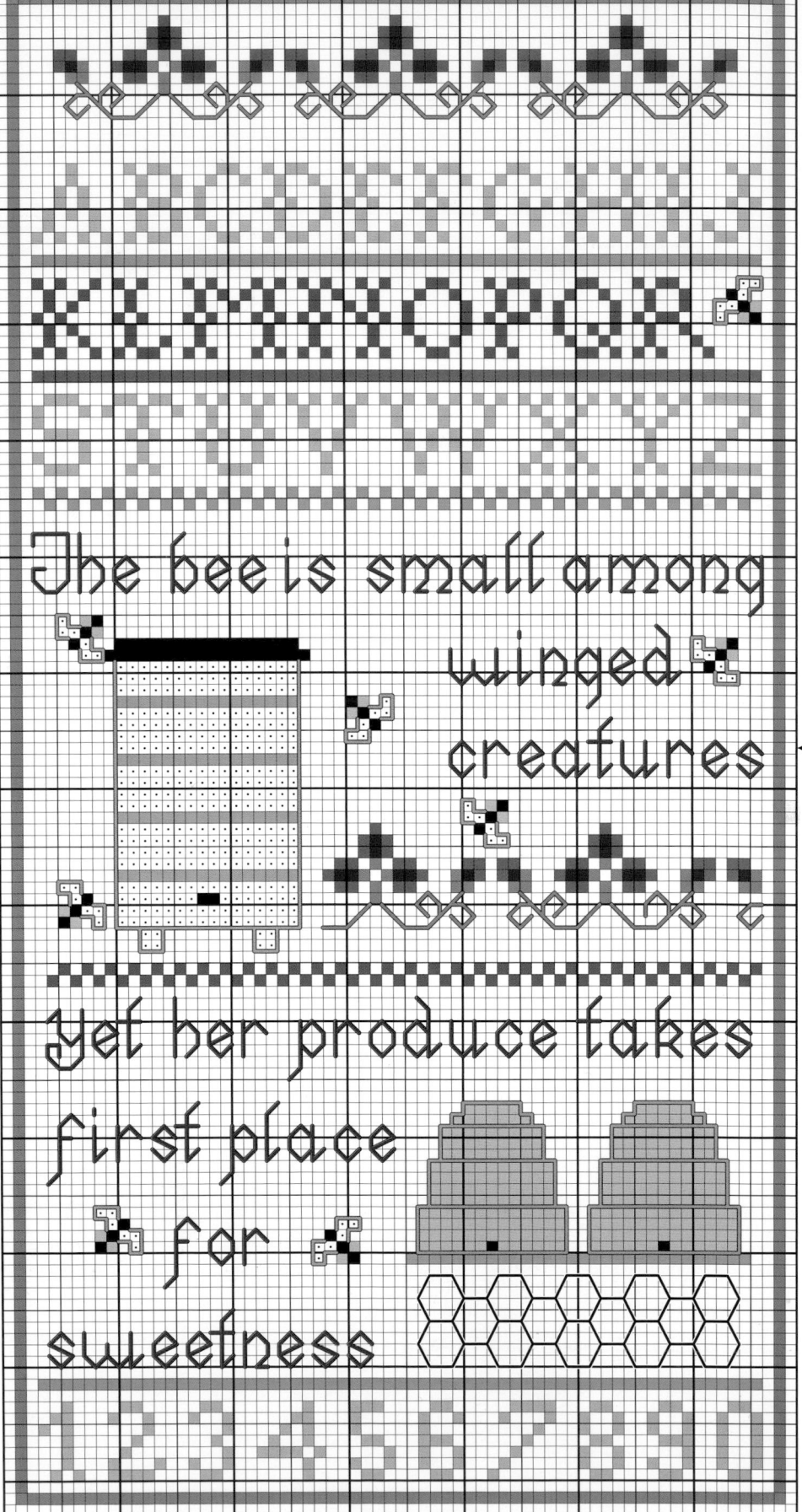

BEEHIVE SAMPLER KEY

DMC stranded cotton

- 310
- 349
- 703
- 799
- 926
- 932
- 3363
- 3705
- 3821
- • BLANC

Backstitch

——— 310
——— 349
——— 926
——— 3363

NOTES

Stitch over two threads of cream 28 count linen with DMC stranded cottons, using two strands for cross stitch and one for backstitch. Embellishments: gold bee charm.

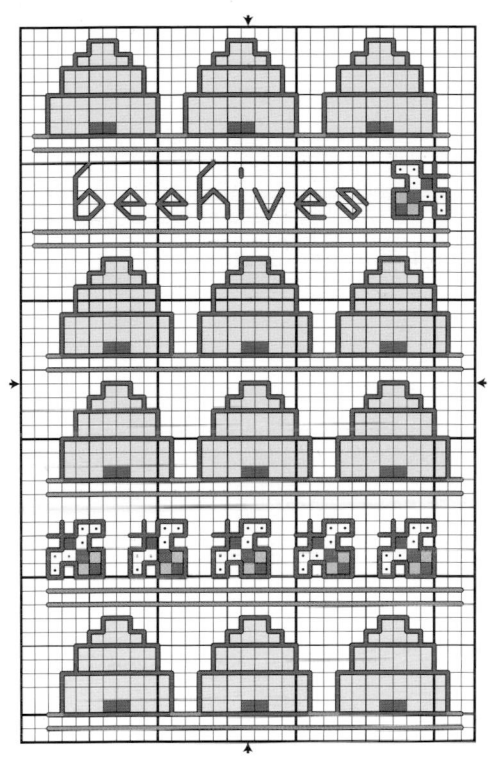

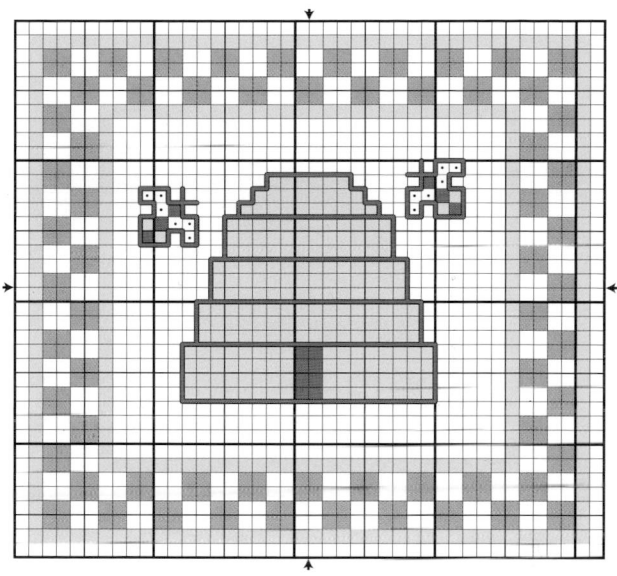

YELLOW BEEHIVE CARD KEY

DMC stranded cotton

				Backstitch
■ *340*		□ *725*		—— *413*
■ *413*		• BLANC		

NOTES

*Stitch over two threads of white 28 count linen with DMC
stranded cottons, using two strands for cross stitch and one
for backstitch.*

BEEHIVES CARD KEY

DMC stranded cotton

			Backstitch
■ *317*	■ *3820*		—— *317*
□ *422*	• BLANC		—— *501*
			—— *840*

NOTES

*Stitch over two threads of sand 28 count linen with DMC
stranded cottons, using two strands for cross stitch and one
for backstitch. Outline the beehives with 317.*

BUTTERFLIES AND BEES TOWEL

I chose this deep green towel to fit the garden theme, but the wide band of butterflies and bees would look very pretty on pastel coloured towels and stunning on bright ones, too. Instead of buying a towel complete with band, you could work the design on an Aida or linen band and stitch it to an ordinary towel.

DESIGN SIZE: 9⅝ x 2½in (24.5 x 6.3cm)
STITCH COUNT: 144 x 35

MATERIALS

❀ One dark green guest towel 11 x 18in
(28 x 46cm) with 14 count cross stitch band
❀ DMC stranded cottons as listed in the key
❀ Size 26 tapestry needle

1 Begin stitching in the centre of the cross stitch band over one block following the chart on pages 100/101. Use two strands of stranded cotton for the cross stitch and one for the backstitch and French knots. Use two strands on the butterflies antennae.

2 When all the stitching is completed, press the towel band carefully.

BUTTERFLY FRIDGE MAGNET

This little butterfly could be stitched in any bright colours, allowing you to match it to your kitchen decor and use up thread leftovers to make lots more of them.

DESIGN SIZE: 1½ x 1½in (4 x 4cm)
STITCH COUNT: 20 x 20

MATERIALS

❀ Vinylweave magnet (Framecraft)
❀ DMC stranded cottons as listed in the key
❀ Size 26 tapestry needle

1 Stitch the butterfly motif from the chart on page 100, using two strands of stranded cotton for the cross stitch and one for the backstitch.

2 When stitching is complete, make up the magnet following the manufacturer's instructions and then cut out carefully round the shape of the butterfly.

INSECT BOX LID

This design fits the lid of a small pine box (shown right), which is available from a firm who specialise in boxes for craft display (see Suppliers). You could also frame this delicate design as a picture.

DESIGN SIZE: 3¾ x 3¾in (9.5 x 9.5cm)
STITCH COUNT: 52 x 52

MATERIALS

❀ 6 x 6in (15 x 15cm) 28 count linen in cream
❀ DMC stranded cottons as listed in the key
❀ Size 26 tapestry needle
❀ Mill Hill purple seed beads (No.00252)
❀ Beading needle
❀ Box 6¼ x 6¼in (16 x 16cm) with a 4 x 4in
(10 x 10cm) lid aperture

1 Find the centre of the fabric and begin stitching here over two fabric threads following the chart on page 100. Use two strands of stranded cotton for the cross stitch and one for the backstitch and French knots.

2 When all the stitching is complete, sew on the seed beads using the beading needle and cream sewing cotton. Press your work carefully and make up the box lid according to the manufacturer's instructions.

These three useful items are decorated with small garden visitors. The Insect Box, Butterflies and Bees Towel and Butterfly Fridge Magnet are all easy to stitch and would make perfect gifts.

beautiful butterflies

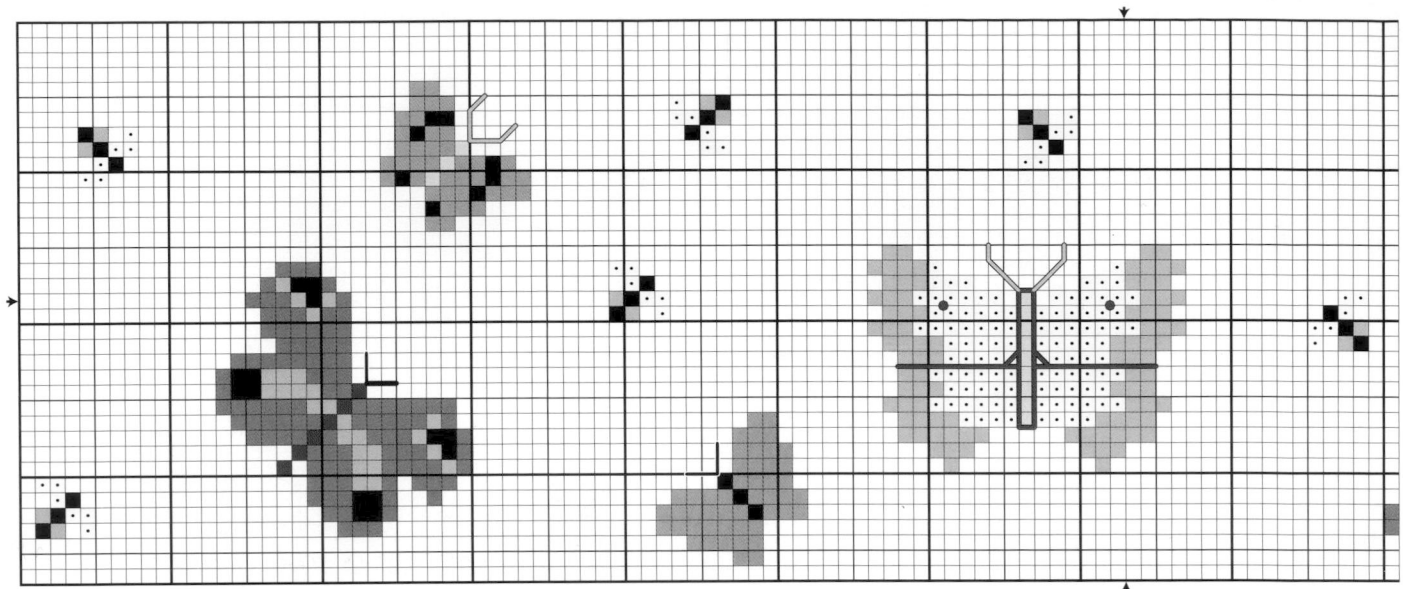

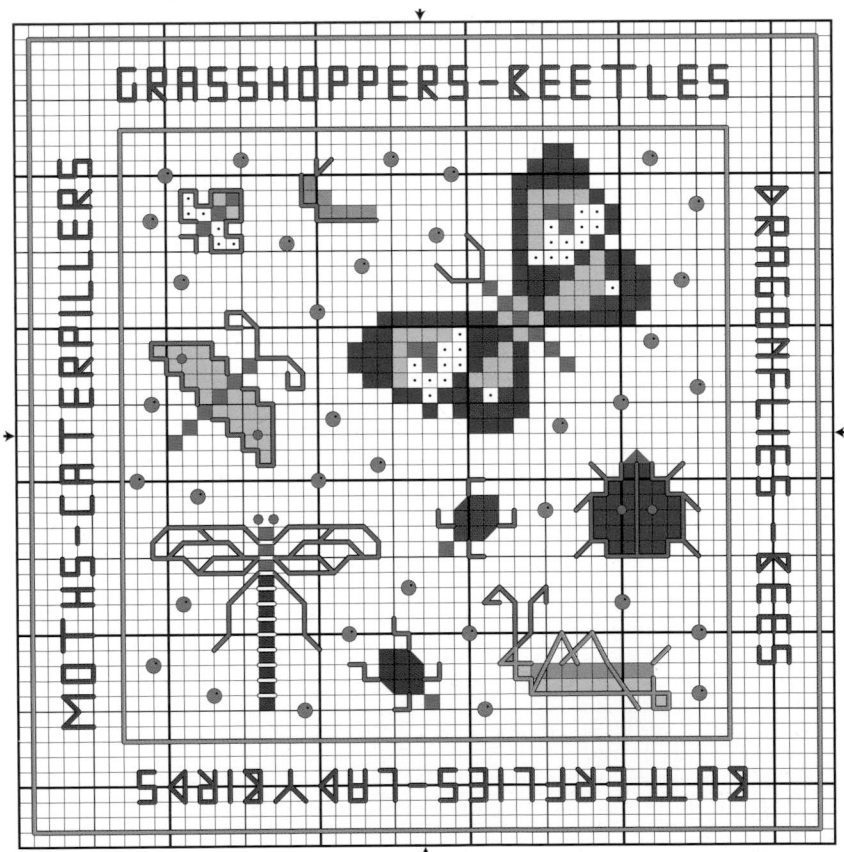

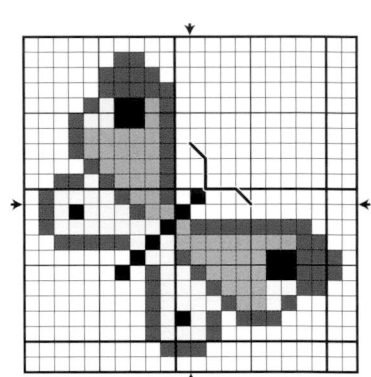

BUTTERFLY FRIDGE MAGNET KEY

DMC stranded cotton		Backstitch	
■ 310	■ 921	——	310
■ 352	□ ECRU		

NOTES

Stitch over one block of vinylweave with DMC stranded cottons, using two strands for cross stitch and one for backstitch.

INSECT BOX LID KEY

DMC stranded cotton		Backstitch		French knots	
■ 312	■ 552	——	367	● 413	
■ 350	■ 3820	——	413		
■ 367	· BLANC	——	552	**Beads**	
■ 413		——	BLANC	● MILL HILL PURPLE SEED BEADS	

NOTES

Stitch over two threads of cream 28 count linen with DMC stranded cottons, using two strands for cross stitch and one for backstitch and French knots.
Embellishments: purple seed beads.

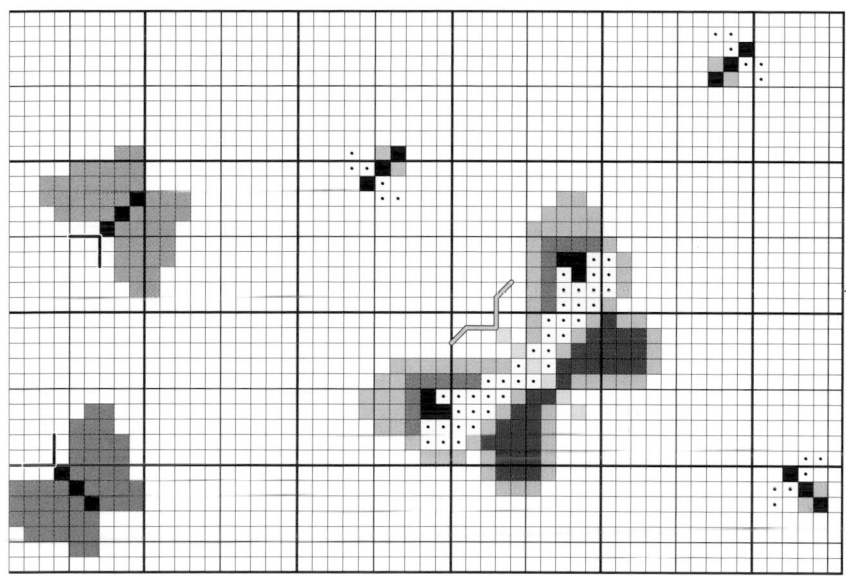

BUTTERFLIES AND BEES TOWEL KEY

DMC stranded cotton

■ 310		▨ 3608	
▨ 351		▨ 3820	
■ 434		· ECRU	
▨ 437			

Backstitch

—— 310
—— 434
—— 437

French knots

● 434

NOTES

Stitch over one block of a 14 count Aida band (in a ready-made towel) with DMC stranded cottons, using two strands for the cross stitch. Use two strands for the backstitch antennae and one strand for remaining backstitch and French knots.

BUTTERFLIES AND LADYBIRDS PICTURE KEY

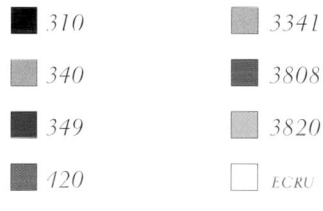

DMC stranded cotton

■ 310		▨ 3341
▨ 340		▨ 3808
■ 349		▨ 3820
▨ 420		□ ECRU
▨ 718		

Backstitch

—— 310
—— 420
—— 3808

French knots

● 310
● 3820

NOTES

Stitch over two threads of white 28 count linen with DMC stranded cottons, using two strands for cross stitch and one for backstitch and French knots.

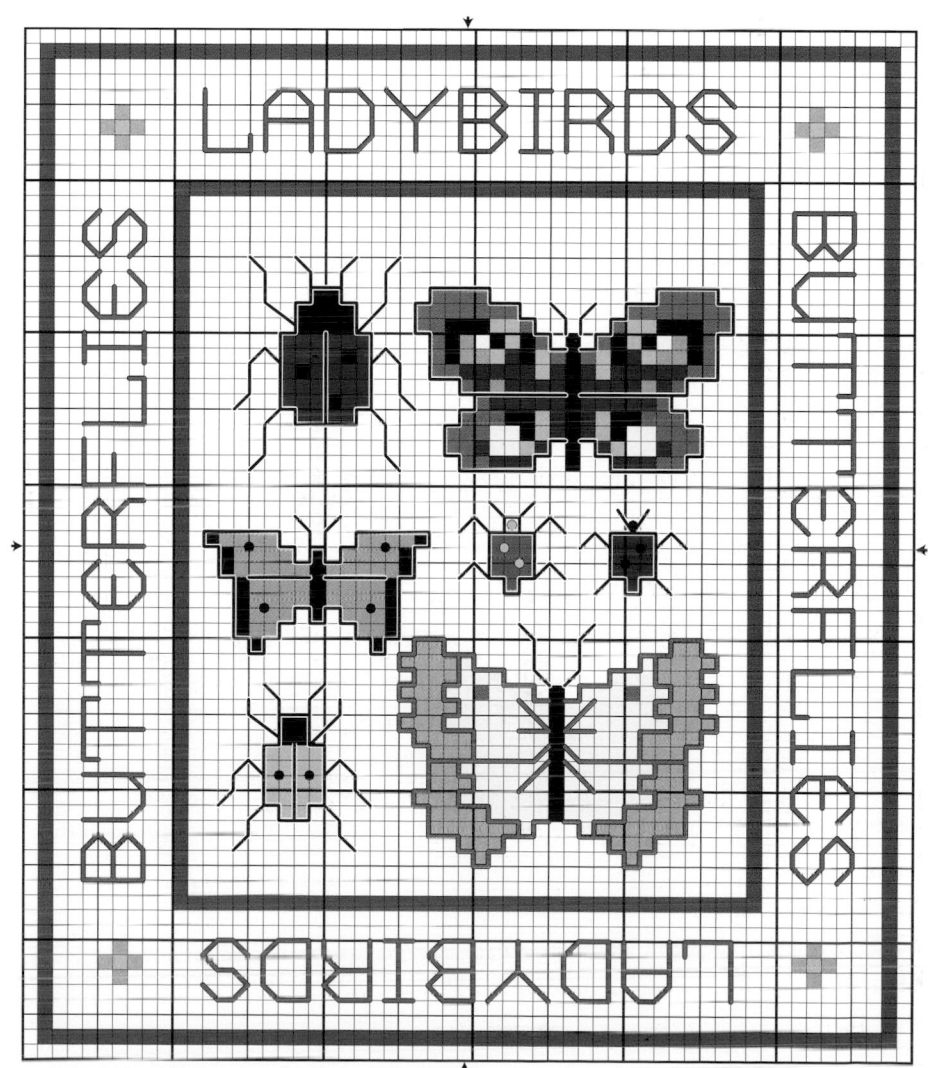

THE FRUIT ORCHARD

Throughout history, orchards have been important not only for their fruit but also for the delights of their blossom, scent and shade on hot summer days. The main orchard fruits in Britain were apples, pears, cherries and plums, followed by mulberries, medlars, walnuts and quince. Soft fruits were grown and any which were not consumed immediately were preserved in jams and jellies, put into syrups and bottled to store for winter time. Favourite soft fruits were, and still are, strawberries, blackberries, raspberries and blackcurrants. The designs in this chapter feature a profusion of all these fruits in various samplers, pictures and a towel border.

APPLE TREE SAMPLER

apple trees

This design is a celebration of apple trees, in the bright reds and greens associated with that fruit. I have added an apple basket button, but there is also a stitched version.

DESIGN SIZE: 6³⁄₁₆ x 7³⁄₁₆in (15.7 x 18.2cm)
STITCH COUNT: 87 x 101

MATERIALS

❀ 12 x 14in (30 x 35cm) 28 count linen in cream
❀ DMC stranded cottons as listed in the key
❀ Size 26 tapestry needle
❀ Apple basket button (Debbie Cripps)

1 Find the centre of the fabric and begin stitching here over two fabric threads, following the chart on page 104, using two strands of stranded cotton for the cross stitch and one strand for the backstitch.

2 When all the stitching is complete, sew on the apple basket button with matching sewing cotton. Sew it on firmly so it remains in the correct place. If you are not using the button you could stitch another apple basket motif from the chart in its place.

3 Finally, press your embroidery carefully and frame it with a suitable frame.

APPLES

Since ancient times apples have been the most popular fruit to eat raw and to use in many recipes, like apple sauce, pies, puddings, flans and to add tartness to savoury dishes. Some English favourites are Bramley's Seedling, Newton Wonder, Annie Elizabeth, Blenheim Orange, Sturmer Pippin, Cox's Orange Pippin, Ribston Pippin and Laxton's Superb. All these varieties will store well for a long time. The fruit should be picked when fully ripe. Apples are best stored in single layers in trays or in boxes and each fruit should be separately wrapped in paper.

APPLE TREE SAMPLER KEY

DMC stranded cotton

- 347
- 350
- 422
- 434
- 703
- 844
- 911
- 3807
- 3818
- 3822
- • BLANC

Backstitch
- ——— 703
- ——— 844

NOTES

Stitch over two threads of cream 28 count linen with DMC stranded cottons, using two strands for cross stitch and one for backstitch. Embellishments: apple basket button.

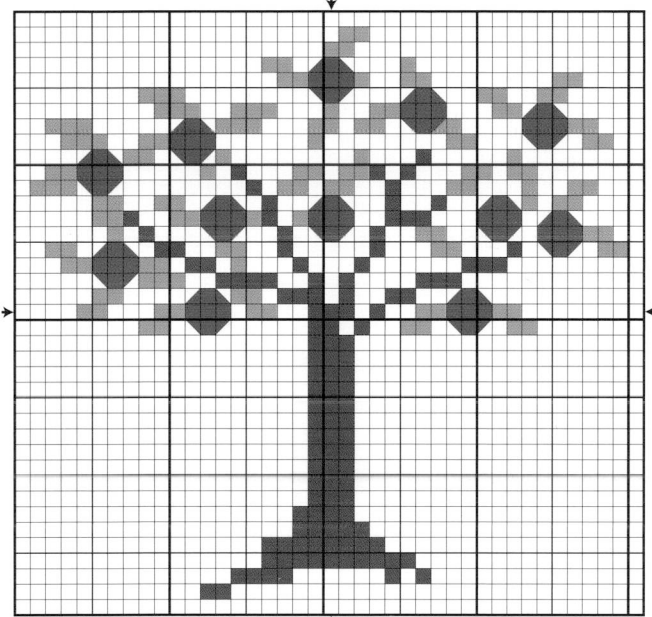

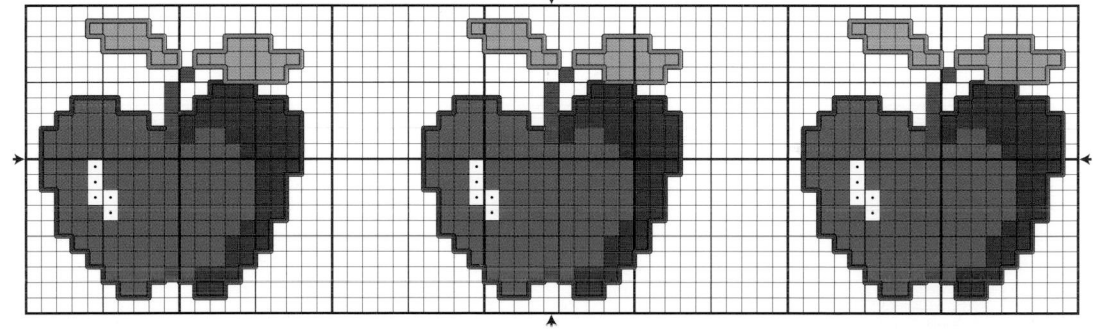

APPLE TREE PICTURE KEY

DMC stranded cotton

- 350
- 434
- 703

NOTES

Stitch over two threads of cream 28 count linen with DMC stranded cottons, using two strands for the cross stitch.

APPLE TEA TOWEL BORDER AND APPLE PICTURE KEY

DMC stranded cotton

- 347
- 350
- 703
- 844
- • BLANC

Backstitch
- ——— 347
- ——— 911

NOTES

Stitch the Tea Towel over one block of a 14 count white Aida band with a red edge. Stitch the Picture over two threads of cream 28 count linen. Use DMC stranded cottons, with two strands for cross stitch and one for backstitch.

APPLE TREE PICTURE

The apple tree in this picture (see photograph opposite) would also make a lovely birthday card, or you could appliqué the cross-stitched picture onto a pot holder to brighten up the kitchen.

DESIGN SIZE: 2⅜ x 2¼in (6.2 x 5.6cm)
STITCH COUNT: 39 x 37

MATERIALS

❀ 6 x 6in (15 x 15cm) 28 count linen in cream
❀ DMC stranded cottons as listed in the key
❀ Size 26 tapestry needle
❀ Bright green frame with 3 x 3in (7.5 x 7.5cm) aperture

1 Find the centre of the fabric and begin stitching over two threads following the chart on page 105, using two strands of stranded cotton for the cross stitch.

2 When all the stitching is complete press your work carefully and frame it.

APPLE TEA TOWEL BORDER

The juicy red apples on this Aida band border look lovely against a bright red tea towel. They would also look good against red or green checked tea towels.

DESIGN SIZE (THREE APPLES): 4½ x 1¼in (11.5 x 3.2cm)
STITCH COUNT (THREE APPLES): 67 x 18

MATERIALS

❀ 2in (5cm) deep Aida band in white with red edge, 22in (55cm) long (or the width of your tea towel)
❀ DMC stranded cottons as listed in the key
❀ Size 26 tapestry needle
❀ Red tea towel

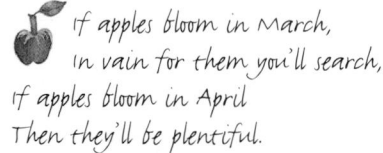

*If apples bloom in March,
In vain for them you'll search,
If apples bloom in April
Then they'll be plentiful.*

1 Fold the Aida band in half and begin stitching from the centre over one block, following the chart on page 105. Work outwards, first one side of the band and then the other. Use two strands of stranded cotton for the cross stitch and one for the backstitch. The gap between each apple is eight blocks, and the apples start three blocks down from the top of the band.

2 When the embroidery is complete, press carefully then pin and sew the band into position on the towel, with matching sewing cotton and small stitches.

APPLE PICTURE

This simple picture takes a single apple motif, turning it into something special by framing it in a bright green frame. You could make it up into a card instead.

DESIGN SIZE: 1⅛ x 1³⁄₁₆in (2.8 x 3cm)
STITCH COUNT: 17 x 18

MATERIALS

❀ 6 x 6in (15 x 15cm) 28 count linen in cream
❀ DMC stranded cottons as listed in the key
❀ Size 26 tapestry needle
❀ Green frame with 2 x 2in (5 x 5cm) aperture

1 Stitch over two threads following the chart on page 105, using two strands of stranded cotton for the cross stitch and one for the backstitch.

2 When all the stitching is complete press your work carefully and frame.

Rosy apples galore in this Apple Tree Picture, Apple Tea Towel Border and little Apple Picture

bountiful harvest

an apple a day

FOUR FRUIT PICTURES

This set of pictures, each featuring a different fruit, was designed to be hung as a group, or could be framed as a set in one frame. Alternatively you could just stitch one picture of your own favourite fruit.

a pair of pears

Pears Picture

DESIGN SIZE: 2⅞ x 2⅞in (7.3 x 7.3cm)
STITCH COUNT: 40 x 40

MATERIALS

❀ 5 x 5in (12.5 x 12.5cm) 28 count linen in cream
❀ DMC stranded cottons as listed in the key
❀ Size 26 tapestry needle

1 Find the centre of the fabric and start stitching here over two fabric threads, following the chart on page 110. Use two strands of stranded cotton for the cross stitch and one for the backstitching and outlining.

2 When all the stitching is complete, press your embroidery carefully and frame.

cherries Picture

DESIGN SIZE: 2⅞ x 2⅞in (7.3 x 7.3cm)
STITCH COUNT: 40 x 40

MATERIALS

❀ 5 x 5in (12.5 x 12.5cm) 28 count linen in cream
❀ DMC stranded cottons as listed in the key
❀ Size 26 tapestry needle

1 Find the centre of the fabric and start stitching here over two fabric threads, following the chart on page 110. Use two strands of stranded cotton for the cross stitch and one for the backstitching and outlining.

2 When all the stitching is complete, press carefully and frame.

COUNTRY SAYINGS

'Walnuts and pears you plant for your heirs.'

'A cherry year, a merry year. A plum year, a dumb year.'

September blow soft 'til the fruit's in the loft.

Peaches Picture

DESIGN SIZE: 2⅞ x 2⅞in (7.3 x 7.3cm)
STITCH COUNT: 40 x 40

MATERIALS

- 5 x 5in (12.5 x 12.5cm) 28 count linen in cream
- DMC stranded cottons as listed in the key
- Size 26 tapestry needle

1 Find the centre of the fabric and start stitching here over two fabric threads, following the chart on page 111. Use two strands of stranded cotton for the cross stitch and one for the backstitching and outlining.

2 When all the stitching is complete, press carefully and frame your picture.

Plums Picture

DESIGN SIZE: 2⅞ x 2⅞in (7.3 x 7.3cm)
STITCH COUNT: 40 x 40

MATERIALS

- 5 x 5in (12.5 x 12.5cm) 28 count linen in cream
- DMC stranded cottons as listed in the key
- Size 26 tapestry needle

1 Find the centre of the fabric and start stitching here over two fabric threads, following the chart on page 111. Use two strands of stranded cotton for the cross stitch and one for the backstitching and outlining.

2 When all the stitching is complete, press carefully and frame your picture.

a plum year

PICKLED PEACHES

In a saucepan dissolve 1kg sugar in 500ml white vinegar. Crush 25g cloves and 25g cinnamon stick, place in a muslin bag, put in the saucepan, then add 2kg peaches and simmer. Remove the peaches when tender and put into preserving jars. Remove the spices and boil the liquid until syrupy. Pour over the fruit and seal.

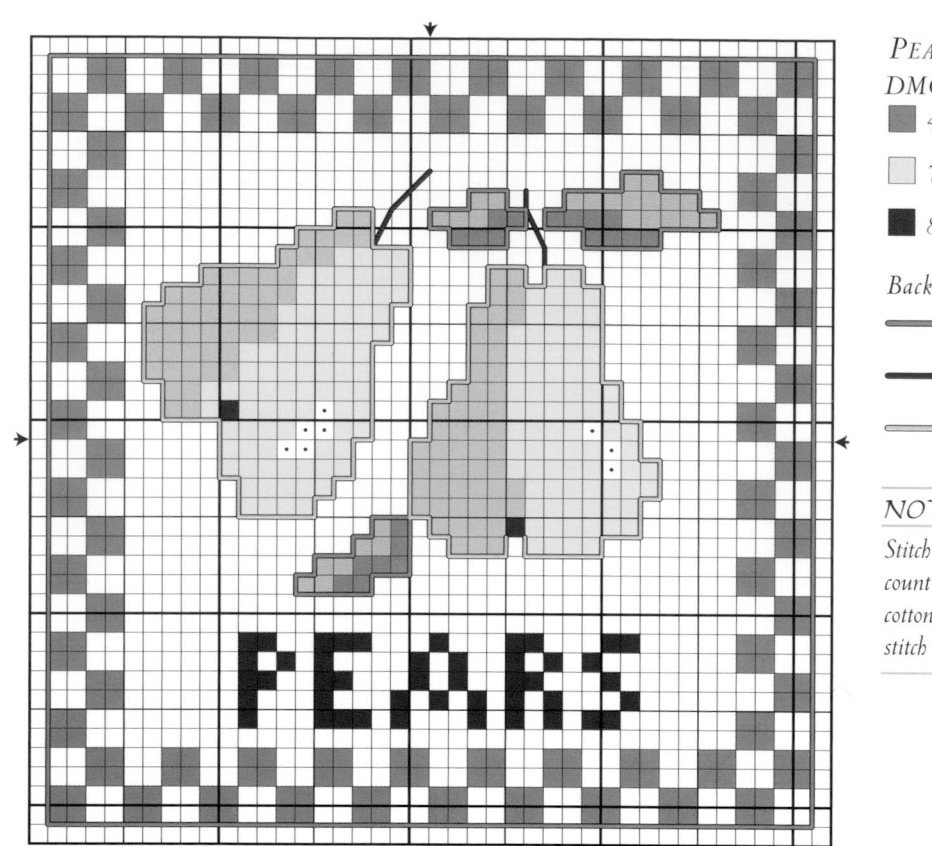

PEARS PICTURE KEY

DMC stranded cotton

▨	470	▨	3348
▨	725	▨	3820
▨	839	·	BLANC

Backstitch

—— 470

—— 839

—— 3820

NOTES

Stitch over two threads of cream 28 count linen with DMC stranded cottons, using two strands for cross stitch and one for backstitch.

CHERRIES PICTURE KEY

DMC stranded cotton

▨	221	▨	3348
▨	309	·	BLANC
▨	470		

Backstitch

—— 221

—— 422

—— 470

NOTES

Stitch over two threads of cream 28 count linen with DMC stranded cottons, using two strands for cross stitch and one for backstitch.

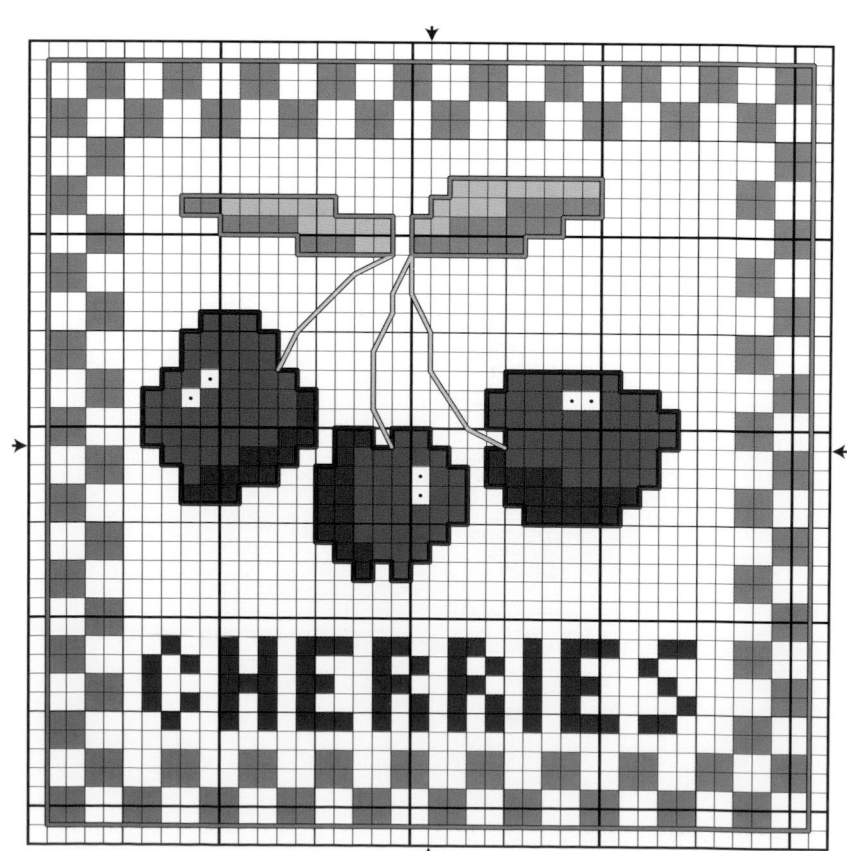

PEACHES PICTURE KEY

DMC stranded cotton

■ 470	■ 3826
■ 976	■ 3827
■ 3348	· BLANC

Backstitch

—— 470

—— 3826

NOTES

Stitch over two threads of cream 28 count linen with DMC stranded cottons, using two strands for cross stitch and one for backstitch.

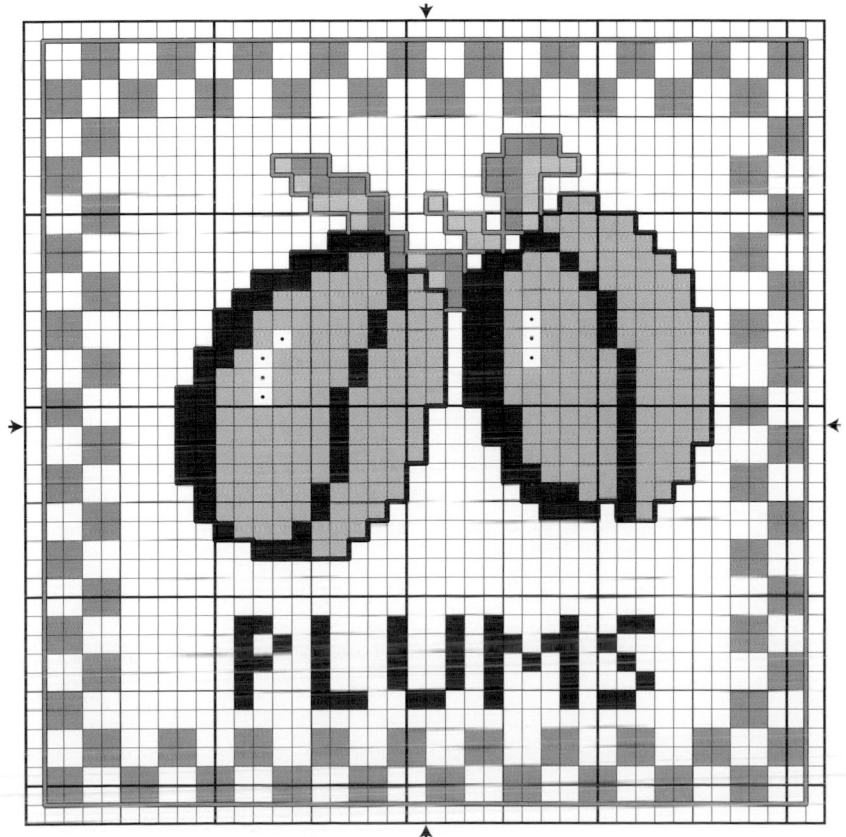

PLUMS PICTURE KEY

DMC stranded cotton

■ 470	■ 3348
■ 550	· BLANC
■ 553	

Backstitch

—— 470

—— 550

NOTES

Stitch over two threads of cream 28 count linen with DMC stranded cottons, using two strands for cross stitch and one for backstitch.

STRAWBERRY SAMPLER

Strawberries are such beautiful and decorative fruits it is no wonder that they have been used by stitchers for centuries in their designs. I decided to use the lovely rayon floss threads for some of the fruits in this design to add sheen and lustre. I also included strawberry buttons and gold bee charms and designed the sampler round an old-fashioned basket tied with a shiny bow.

DESIGN SIZE: 4 x 7½in (10 x 19cm)
STITCH COUNT: 56 x 105

MATERIALS

- 8 x 13in (20 x 33cm) 28 count linen in antique white
- DMC stranded cottons as listed in the key
- DMC rayon threads as listed in the key
- Size 26 tapestry needle
- Two Mill Hill strawberry buttons (American Country Cross Stitch)
- Two gold bee charms (Heritage Stitchcraft)

1 Find the centre of the fabric and begin stitching here over two fabric threads following the chart on page 114. For the cross stitch use two strands of stranded cotton and one for the rayon threads. Use one strand for the backstitching and outlining.

succulent strawberries

STRAWBERRY SHORTCAKE

250g plain flour
3 teaspoons baking powder
1 tablespoon castor sugar
60g butter
150ml milk
1/2 teaspoon salt
500g strawberries
2 tablespoons castor sugar
250ml double cream

Sift flour, baking powder, sugar and salt in a mixing bowl. Rub in butter until the mixture resembles fine breadcrumbs. Add milk and work into a dough. Knead on a floured board, then divide in half and put in two buttered 20cm cake tins. Bake in hot oven for ten minutes till golden, then cool on a rack. Slice the strawberries and sugar well. Whip the cream until thick. Arrange the strawberries and cream on the shortcakes, sprinkling with sugar.

2 When all the stitching is complete, sew on the buttons and charms with matching thread if you are using them. If you are not using the button, stitch the strawberry motif from the chart instead. Press the work carefully and frame.

STRAWBERRY SAMPLER KEY

DMC stranded cotton/rayon

■	367
■	413
■	420
■	422
□	726
⊡	BLANC
■	30351 RAYON
■	30498 RAYON
□	30957 RAYON

Backstitch

——	367
——	413
——	3721
——	BLANC

NOTES

Stitch over two threads of antique white 28 count linen with DMC stranded cottons, using two strands for cross stitch and one for backstitch. Use one strand of the rayon threads throughout. Backstitch the flower tendrils in 367. Outline the bees, fruit and basket in 413.
Embellishments: two strawberry buttons, two gold bee charms.

WINTER BERRY BASKET

This bright display of seasonal berries would make an attractive little picture or a festive card. You could stitch the berries in a shiny rayon floss if you like.

seasonal berries

DESIGN SIZE: 3¹⁄₁₆ x 3in (8 x 7.5cm)
STITCH COUNT: 45 x 43

MATERIALS

* 6 x 6in (15 x 15cm) 28 count linen in antique white
* DMC stranded cottons as listed in the key
* Size 26 tapestry needle
* Gold bow charm (Debbie Cripps)

1 Find the centre of the fabric and begin stitching here over two fabric threads following the chart below. When working the cross stitch use two strands of stranded cotton. Use one strand for the backstitching.

2 When all stitching is complete, sew on the gold bow charm if using it, then press your work and frame.

BERRY FRUITS

The gooseberry, raspberry and roses, all three, with strawberries under them trimly agree.
Thomas Tusser

WINTER BERRY BASKET KEY

DMC stranded cotton

■ 333		■ 911		Backstitch	
■ 340		□ 3747		▬▬	340
■ 349		■ 3799		▬▬	470
■ 470		□ ECRU		▬▬	911
				▬▬	3799

NOTES

Stitch over two threads of antique white 28 count linen with DMC stranded cottons, using two strands for cross stitch and one for backstitch.
Embellishments: gold bow charm.

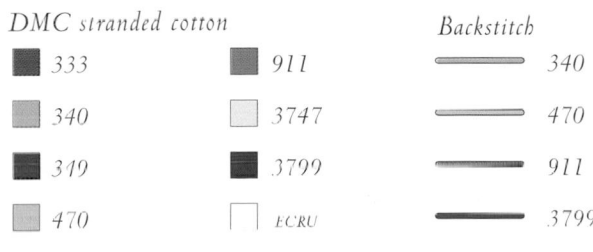

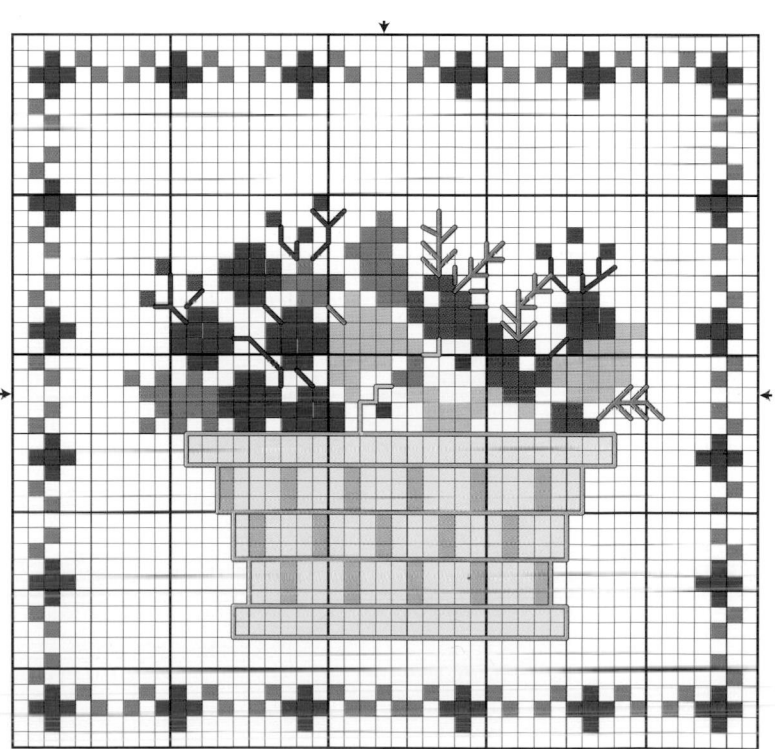

GARDEN ALPHABET

🌿 *This bright garden alphabet design brings together many of the themes explored throughout the book into one large picture. Many of the letters and their illustrations could be taken out, stitched quickly and used for smaller projects. Just a few examples of these are described overleaf and shown in the photograph on page 118.*

GARDEN ALPHABET

DESIGN SIZE: 8⅝ x 8⅝in (21.8 x 21.8cm)
STITCH COUNT: 121 x 121

MATERIALS

* 11 x 11in (28 x 28cm) 28 count linen in cream
* DMC stranded cottons as listed in the key
* Size 26 tapestry needle
* Four gold dragonfly charms (Heritage Stitchcraft)
* Mill Hill ladybird button (American Country Cross Stitch)

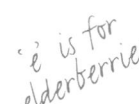

'e' is for elderberries

1 Find the centre of the fabric and begin stitching here over two fabric threads following the chart on pages 120/121, using two strands of stranded cotton for the cross stitch and one strand for the backstitch.

2 When all the stitching is complete, sew on the charms and button if you are using them. If you are not using the button, stitch the ladybird motif from the chart instead. To finish, press your work carefully and frame.

SMALL DESIGNS FROM THE GARDEN ALPHABET

The individual letters and their illustrations from the Garden Alphabet could be used in many ways on all kinds of objects and a few examples are shown here. Use the Garden Alphabet chart on pages 120/121. Why not try stitching the separate elements of the chart and displaying them in cards, coasters, mugs or paper weights (see Suppliers).

DESIGN SIZE FOR EACH ALPHABET SQUARE:
1⅞ x 1⅞in (4.7 x 4.7cm)
STITCH COUNT FOR EACH ALPHABET SQUARE: 25 x 25

ABC Picture

The first three letters of the Garden Alphabet are stitched on cream 14 count stitching paper and are mounted in a ready-made modern frame, ideal to decorate a young child's bedroom.

M for Marigold card

This attractive card with a circular aperture perfectly displays the marigold design from the Garden Alphabet, stitched on cream 14 count stitching paper.

R for Radish Fridge Magnet

This design is first stitched on a 14 count vinylweave magnet from Framecraft and then cut out.

v for violet

v for violet Scissors Keeper

This design is stitched on 28 count white linen and made into a scissors keeper (see Techniques page 125), edged with a multicoloured twisted cord (see page 125).

x for Xmas Rose Tag

This little gift tag uses a Christmas rose image stitched onto 11 count red Aida and is finished off with a silver cord.

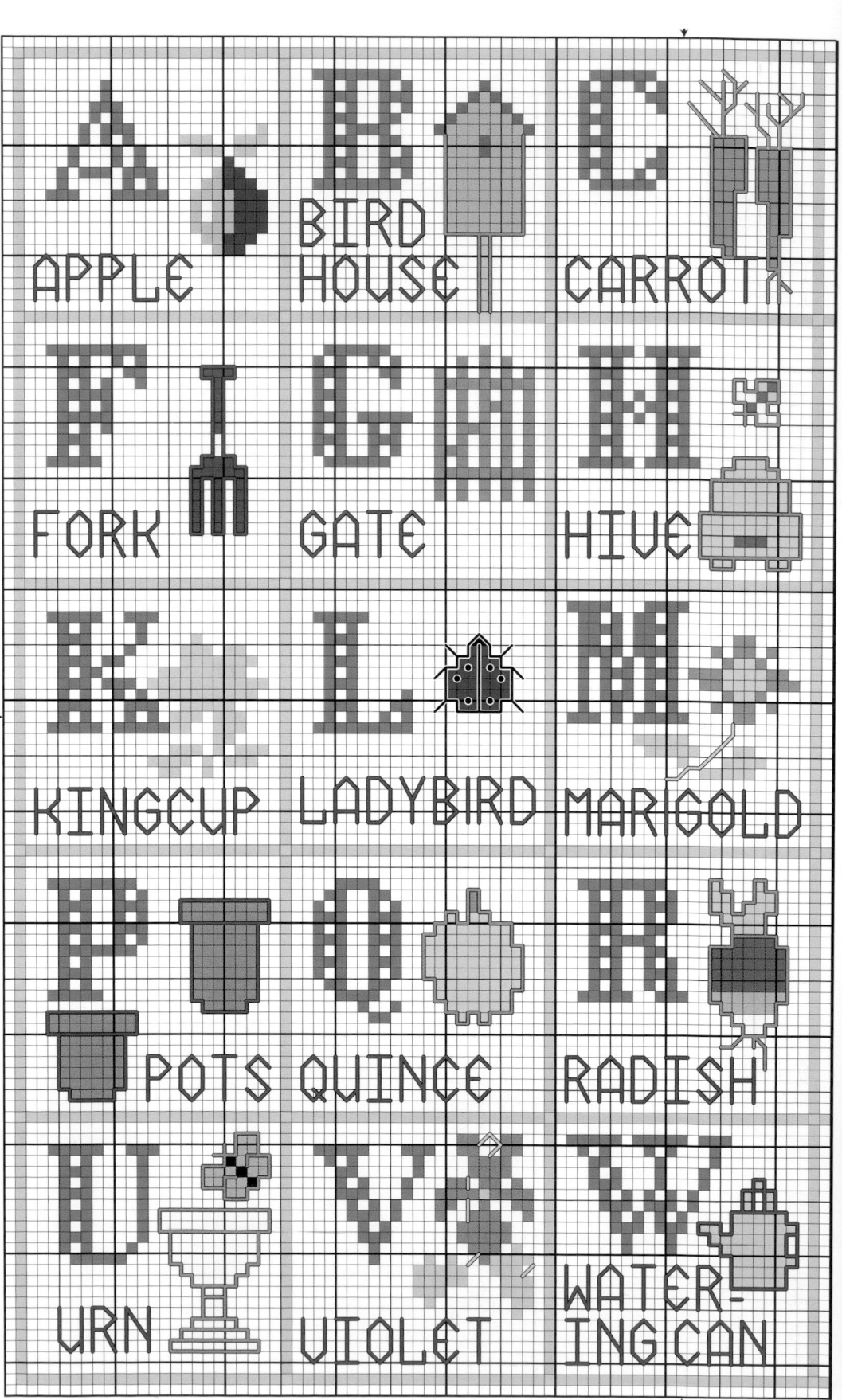

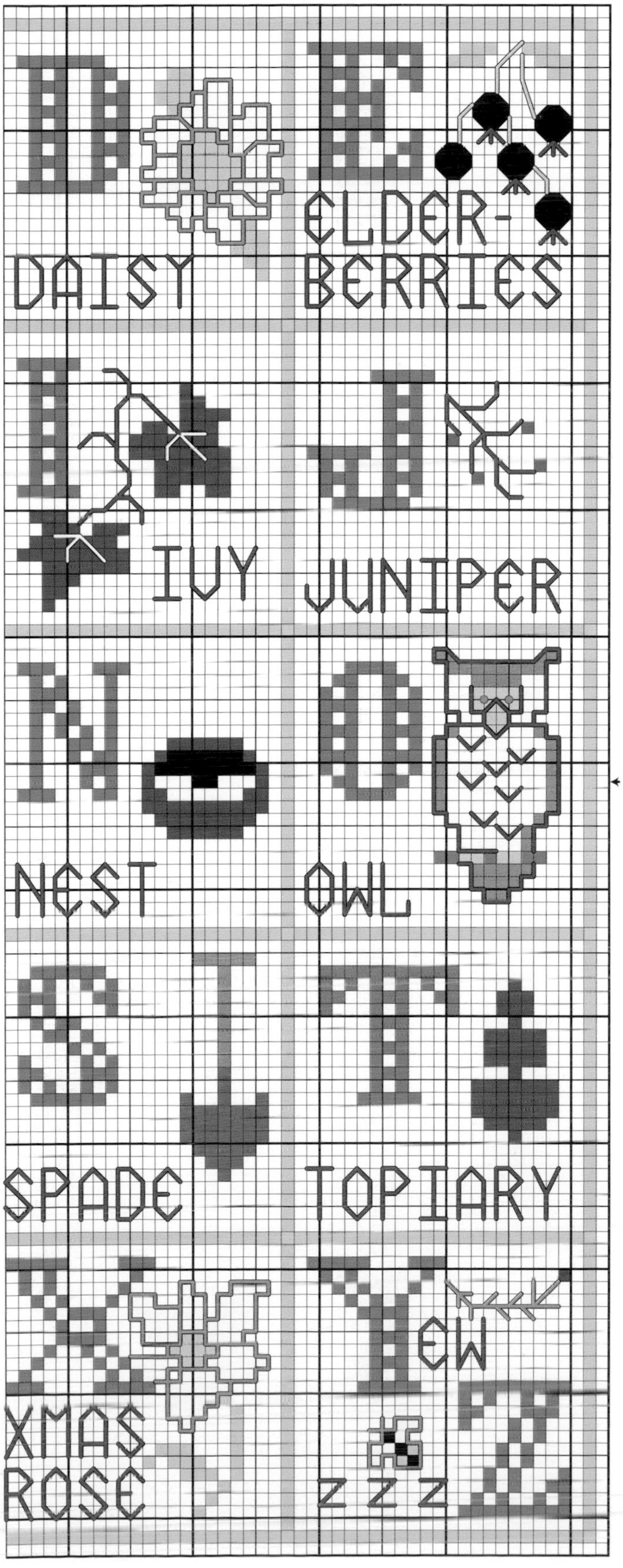

GARDEN ALPHABET KEY

DMC stranded cotton

■	310	■	718
■	349	■	722
■	351	■	841
■	413	■	911
■	501	■	3608
■	553	■	3820
■	611	□	ECRU
■	704		

Backstitch

——	310	——	841
——	501	——	911
——	611	——	ECRU
——	703		

French knots

●	310
●	841

NOTES

Stitch over two threads of cream 28 count linen with DMC stranded cottons, using two strands for cross stitch and one for backstitch.
Embellishments: ladybird button and four gold dragonfly charms.

BASIC TECHNIQUES

This section contains all the basic techniques you will need to work any of the projects

in the book and should be particularly useful to beginners.

WORKING THE STITCHES

There are no complicated stitches to master: all of those used within the projects are described here, accompanied by simple diagrams. For American readers, cotton = floss.

Starting and Finishing

It is always a good idea to start and finish work correctly, to create the neatest effect and avoid ugly bumps and threads trailing across the back of work.

To start off a length of thread, knot one end, then push the needle through to the back of the fabric, about 1¼in (3cm) from your intended starting point, leaving the knot on the right side. Stitch towards the knot, securing the thread at the back of the fabric as you go. When the thread is secure, cut off the knot.

To finish off a thread (or start new threads), simply weave the needle and thread into the back of several worked stitches and then trim off neatly.

Backstitching and Outlining

Backstitch is indicated on the charts by a solid coloured line. It can be worked on its own, such as for lettering, or on top of other stitches for detail and as

an outline around areas of completed cross stitches to add definition. Most backstitch is worked with one strand of thread.

To work backstitch, bring the needle up through the fabric at I (see Fig I), then take it down at 2. Bring it back up at 3 and then down at I. Repeat the process to make the next stitch. This produces short stitches at the front of the work and longer ones at the back.

Blanket Stitch

This is a variable and useful stitch, perfect for creating a decorative edging as in the vegetable seed packets on the apron on page 39.

Start by bringing the thread out on the lower line shown in Fig 2. Re-insert the needle at I on the upper line and out again at 2, with the thread under the needle point so a loop is formed.

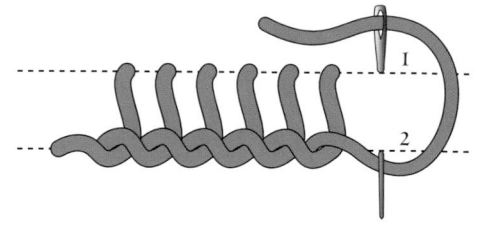

Fig 2

Cross Stitch

This is the main stitch used throughout the projects and each complete cross stitch is represented on the charts by a coloured square. The cross stitches in this book are generally worked over two threads of evenweave (linen) or one block of blockweave (Aida), unless otherwise stated.

A cross stitch is worked in two stages: a diagonal stitch is worked over two threads (or one block), then a second diagonal stitch is worked over the first stitch in the opposite direction, forming a cross (see Fig 3).

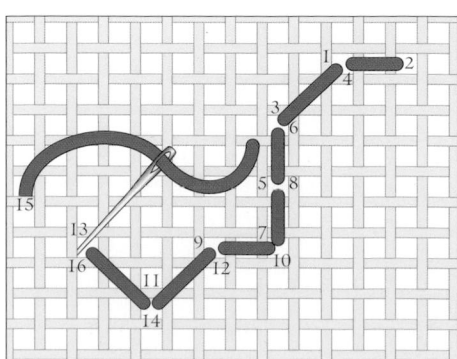

Fig 1

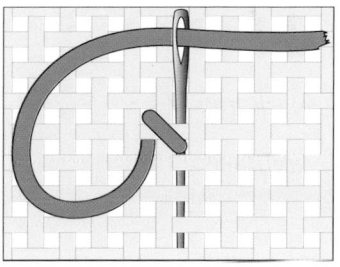

Fig 3 A single cross stitch

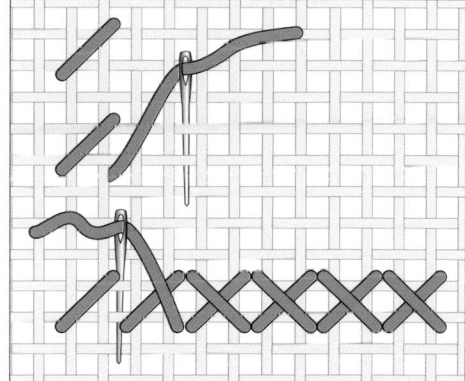

Fig 4 Cross stitches worked in rows

If you have a large area to cover, you may prefer to work the cross stitches in rows. Work a row of half cross stitches in one direction, then work back in the opposite direction with the diagonal stitches needed to complete each cross stitch (see Fig 4). The upper stitches of all the crosses should lie in the same direction to produce a neat effect.

French Knot

This is a useful little stitch and may be used in addition to cross stitch to add texture and emphasis. In this book they are usually work with one or two

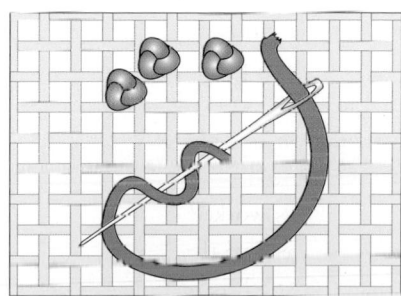

Fig 5

strands of thread and are shown on the charts by a small coloured circle.

To work a French knot, bring the needle up to the right side of the fabric, hold the thread down with your left thumb (if right-handed) and wind the thread around the needle twice. Still holding the thread taut, put the needle through to the back of the work, one thread or part of a block away from the entry point (see Fig 5). If you want bigger knots, add more thread to the needle.

Half Cross Stitch

This is simply one half of a cross stitch, with the diagonal facing the same way as the upper stitches of each complete cross stitch (see Fig 6).

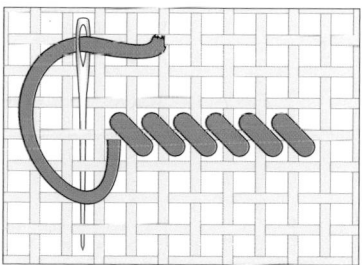

Fig 6

Three-quarter Cross Stitch

This is a part or fractional stitch useful for adding definition to a design and creating smoother curves or circles. Three-quarter cross stitch is shown on the charts by a coloured triangle within a grid square.

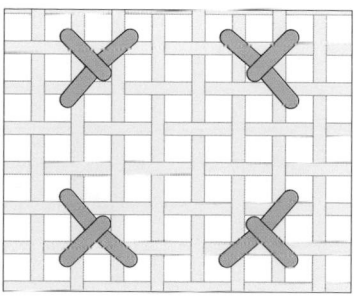

Fig 7

To work three-quarter cross stitch, work a half cross stitch, then add a quarter stitch in the opposite direction, bringing the needle down in the centre of the half cross stitch already worked (see Fig 7).

CARING FOR FINISHED WORK

Cross stitch embroidery can be washed and ironed, though great care should be taken if the work features delicate ceramic buttons. Make sure it is colourfast first, then wash with bleach-free soap in hand-hot water, squeezing gently but never rubbing or wringing. Rinse in plenty of cold or lukewarm water and dry naturally.

To iron cross stitch embroidery, use a hot setting on a steam iron. Cover the ironing board with a thick layer of towelling and place the stitching on this, right side down. Press the fabric firmly but avoid any charms, buttons or metallic threads used.

MOUNTING AND FRAMING EMBROIDERY

It really is best to take large samplers and pictures to a professional framer, where you will be able to choose from a wide variety of mounts and frames that will best enhance your work. The framer will be able to lace and stretch the fabric correctly and cut any surrounding mounts accurately.

If you are mounting work into commercial products, such as box lids, follow the manufacturer's instructions. For small pieces of work, back with lightweight iron-on interfacing to prevent the fabric wrinkling, and then mount.

If you intend to mount the work yourself, use acid-free mounting board in a colour that will not show through the embroidery. Cut the board to fit inside your picture frame and allow for the thickness of the fabric pulled over the edges of the board. Mount using the taping or lacing method.

Taping Method

Place the cut board on the reverse of the work in the position required. Starting from the centre of one of the longest edges, fold the fabric over the board and

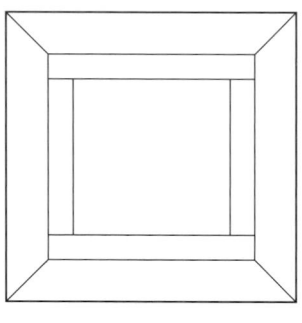

Fig 8

pin through the fabric into the edge of the board to keep the fabric from moving. Check it is in the correct place with no wrinkles or bumps, then stick the work in place using strips of double-sided adhesive tape, removing the pins once finished (see Fig 8).

Lacing Method

Pin the work in place on the board, then working from the centre and using long lengths of strong thread, lace backwards and forwards across the gap (see Fig 9).

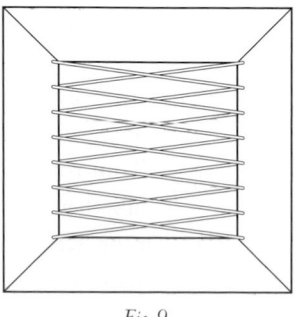

Fig 9

MAKING EMBROIDERY UP INTO A CARD

There are many lovely card mounts available today. They are pre-folded with three sections, the middle one having a window for your embroidery.

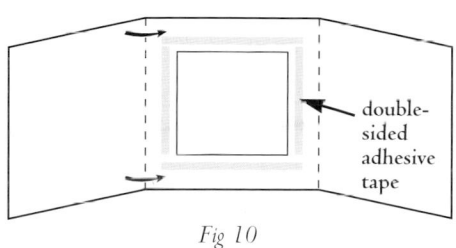

Fig 10

First make sure your embroidery looks good in the window space, then trim your design to the correct size to fit. Position small lengths of double-sided adhesive tape around the window area then remove the backing from the tape. Lay the card on top of the embroidery so that it shows neatly through the window and press into place. Fold the third of the card to cover the back of the embroidery, ensuring that the card opens correctly before securing with more double-sided tape.

MAKING A PINCUSHION OR SCISSORS KEEPER

A piece of embroidery is easily made into a pincushion or scissors keeper and makes an attractive and useful gift. Sachets and small cushions can be made using the same method.

Once your embroidery is complete, take a second piece of fabric the same size (it could be the same type of fabric or a contrasting one) and place the pieces right sides together. Sew round three sides, by hand or machine, some distance away from the last row of stitching, say two threads. Trim the excess fabric and clip the corners to reduce bulk, then turn the right way out. Stuff the pincushion or scissors keeper with polyester filling and slipstitch closed the final side. Sachets can be stuffed with herbs or pot pourri.

MAKING A TWISTED CORD

Many projects are beautifully finished off by the addition of a twisted cord that reflects the colours used in the embroidery. Success in making an even and tightly twisted cord depends on keeping the threads taut at all times.

Cut the required number of lengths of stranded cotton – as a rough guide this length needs to be about three times longer than the finished length required. Knot the lengths together at one end and loop this around a door handle or ask a friend to hold it. Knot the other ends of the strands together and pass a pencil through the loop. Keeping the thread taut, wind the pencil round and round so that the thread twists, eventually coiling around itself. Now carefully bring the two knotted ends together so that both halves of the thread twist around one another. Gently pull and ease the cord until it is evenly twisted, then knot the ends together to prevent them from unravelling. Trim the ends beyond the knots. If required, you can leave about ½in (1.25cm) beyond the knots and tease these out with a pin to make mini tassels.

Fig 11

To make a two- or three-colour twisted cord, simply start with groups of different coloured threads of the required length, bunched together.

SUPPLIERS

If you contact suppliers by post, please remember to enclose a stamped self-addressed envelope.

AMERICAN COUNTRY CROSS STITCH COMPANY
140 Seafield Road, Southbourne, Bournemouth, Dorset BH6 BJL
Tel: 01202 434290
For all **Mill Hill** *buttons,* **Debbie Mumm** *buttons and other folk-art supplies. (See also Framecraft Ltd.)*

DEE FINE ARTS
182 Telegraph Road, Heswall, Wirral CH60 0AJ
Tel: 0151 3426657
For expert embroidery and picture framing.

DMC CREATIVE WORLD
Pullman Road ,Wigston, Leicester L48 2DY
Tel: 0116 281 1040 (call for local stockists)
Fax: 0116 281 3592
For a massive range of threads, fabrics and needlework supplies.

FABRIC FLAIR
Tel: 01985 214 466 (call for local stockists)
For fabrics, stitching paper, charms, beads and general needlework supplies.

FRAMECRAFT LTD
372–376 Summer Lane, Hockley, Birmingham B19 3QA
Tel: 0121 212 0551
Fax: 0121 212 0552
For charms from **Creative Beginnings***, some* **Mill Hill** *buttons,* **Debbie Mumm** *buttons and a wide range of ready-made items.*

FROM DEBBIE CRIPPS
31 Lower Whitelands, Radstock, Bath BA3 3JW
www.debbiecripps.co.uk
For all Flower Pot buttons, other buttons and charms and embroidery supplies.

HERITAGE STITCHCRAFT
Redbrook Lane, Brereton, Rugely, Staffordshire WS15 1QU
Tel: 01899 575256
For **Just Nan** *bee and dragonfly charms and other needlework supplies.*

JOHN LEWIS
Branches in many towns and cities.
For general haberdashery – tea towels, lace, ribbons etc.

LITTLE BOXES
Tel (mobile): 0771 0269654
www.littleboxes.co.uk
For wooden boxes with special recess in the lid to take embroidery.

VOIRREY EMBROIDERY CENTRE
Brimstage Hall, Wirral CH63 6JA
Tel: 0151 342 3514
Fax: 0151 342 5161
For embroidery supplies, books and wonderful exhibitions.

WILLOW FABRICS
27 Willow Green, Knutsford WA16 6AX
Tel: 01565 872 225
Fax: 01565 872 239
For linen, evenweave, **Caron** *threads,* **Mill Hill** *beads,* **Charles Craft** *embroidery items and many other supplies.*

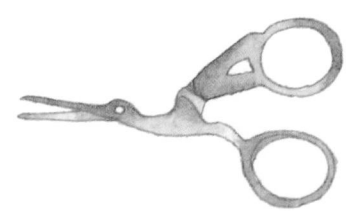

ACKNOWLEDGEMENTS

Thanks to everyone at David & Charles Publishers, especially Cheryl Brown, Brenda Morrison, Sue Cleave, Jennifer Proverbs and Kirsten Evans – and everyone else who worked so hard behind the scenes to produce and promote this book.

A special thank you to Lin Clements for not only editing the text in her usual thorough way, but also charting most of the designs too – beautifully and without a single cross word! Thanks also to Ethan Danielson for his excellent charting. Thank you to David Johnson for the superb photography.

Thanks to everyone at the wonderful Voirrey Embroidery Centre. Thank you to Cara Ackerman and DMC Creative World for continual supplies of lovely thread. And finally thanks as always to my family and friends who are so supportive and encouraging, especially my husband David and daughters Sarah and Rosie.

INDEX